JUDO:
Basic Principles

by

ERIC DOMINY

Illustrated by Peter Johnson

Table of Contents

CHAPTER I
Introduction

In the course of long experience of judo, both as student and instructor, I have been unable to find a book on the subject that caters exclusively to the beginner. Indeed, even my own previous books were intended for both beginners and advanced performers. The recent rapid increase in the number of new enthusiasts, however, has now made the need for such a book imperative, and it is in an attempt to meet this requirement that the present book is offered.

The instruction it contains is based on the highly successful lessons organized by the London Judo Society, the techniques described being grouped for purposes of easy reference under their appropriate heads—Breakfalls, Hand Throws, Foot Throws, etc. I chose this arrangement instead of the more usual method of arbitrarily drawing up a series of progressive lessons, because I believed it would be the form of presentation most acceptable to the greatest number of readers. Most clubs have their own ideas as to the order in which the various judo techniques should be studied, and it is obviously desirable that club members should adhere to whatever program is prescribed. The pattern of this book is designed to meet this requirement and at the same time to allow the enthusiast to add to his knowledge of judo, both in general terms and in close detail.

Nevertheless, for those readers who desire guidance on this most important subject, I have included two recommended schedules of instruction which have been proved and successfully followed by a great many newcomers to the sport. Whether the reader decides to follow either of these schedules, or such modification of them as may be otherwise recommended, is of no particular significance. What does matter is that he should learn to walk before he attempts to run. The man who engages in judo in a cheerfully haphazard fashion is doomed to disappointment from the start. There is no short cut to proficiency, and anybody who attempts the advanced techniques before he is thoroughly grounded in the more elementary ones becomes a nuisance and a danger to both himself and his opponents.

Because enthusiasm can be quickly damped and style permanently spoiled by the attempted use of the more violent counters in the early days of initiation, I have omitted all reference to them and also to throws which enable a stronger man to overcome a weaker opponent solely by virtue of his greater strength. The beginner does not need such techniques and it is much better that he should not experiment with them until he has acquired a very fair measure of experience and proficiency.

I have, however, included the Sacrifice Throws, though somewhat against my better judgment, because these are not throws I would normally recommend to the novice. This is a personal view with which not all instructors agree, and consequently some schools include limited instruction in the Sacrifice Throws in their classes of novice training. Thus, there is always the possibility of a beginner unexpectedly coming up against a Sacrifice Throw early in his career. Believing that to be forewarned is to be forearmed, I have thought it best to set aside my own preference in this matter and to put the reader in the picture with a description of the Stomach Throw.

In two cases I have transferred throws from the groups to which they properly belong to other groups to which they have a more marked affinity of character. The two examples of this are the Body Drop and the Shoulder Throw. Both these are Hand Throws, but in this book, they appear in the Leg Throw and Shoulder Throw groups respectively. I have done this because many beginners find these two throws easier to learn as Leg and Shoulder Throws than as Hand Throws.

The reader will note that I have had no hesitation in repeating certain points of instruction ad nauseam throughout the book. This is because the points emphasized are the fundamental principles on which all judo is based and therefore cannot be repeated too often.

Finally, let me conclude these opening remarks with a few words of advice. Do your best to remain receptive to instruction at all times. Everybody suffers brief periods of "staleness," of course, but try to keep them as short as possible. Staleness is a mental rather than physical failing, and at such moments it is desperately easy to persuade yourself that you "know it all." The answer to this is that you do not know it all and never will. By the time that you reach the Black Belt grade you will begin to realize how little you really know. But what fun you will have had in the learning of that little !

CHAPTER II
Concerning Judo Generally

Some Popular Fallacies

A great many words, some of them nonsense, have been written about the esoteric side of judo. Some writers apparently wish to give the impression that judo is a mixture of Buddhism, Yoga and Shintoism leavened by no more than a trace of sport. Don't be misled by this. Judo is an art, admittedly, but it is a fighting art with a major element of first-class competitive sport. The mysticism with which it has been popularly endowed comes from its eastern origin when it was exclusively a Japanese pursuit. Since then the practice of judo has extended to most of the countries of the world, where it has become an integral part in the framework of their sporting activities. Thus, while acknowledging Japan as the originating nation, each country has its own officiating body to regulate and organize the sport within its own boundaries.

For this reason, the names of the throws, locks and holds have passed into the languages of the countries practicing them; but only as terms of convenience. In all serious judo circles the Japanese terminology is observed, whatever the language of the country. And with excellent reason, for only by retaining a common language can teaching remain standard and universally comprehensible to all the judo nations of the world.

Other popular generalizations one often hears are "judo is a gentle art in which strength is not required," "you use your opponent's strength," "the secret is mental and physical balance." Such statements can also be misleading if taken too literally. It is true that a concept of judo is "giving way to strength," but, given equal skill, it is equally true that the stronger man will usually win in judo just as he will in any other fighting sport. Strength is, of course, needed, but more important is the knowledge of how to use it. The secret is to oppose your opponent's strength by applying your own in the direction in which he is weakest and least able to combat it.

The Judo Outfit

It is an old saying, but a true one, that a job that is worth doing is worth doing well. This is particularly true of all matters pertaining to judo; half-measures will get you nowhere. Therefore, although there is no technical reason why any suitable old clothes should not be used, only the correct judo wear is acceptable and should be worn on every occasion. Apart from the fact that most clubs insist on the traditional dress being worn, there is a personal satisfaction to be gained from turning out clean and correctly clad. Other considerations apart, one is uncomfortably conspicuous if one is not properly dressed, and any such feeling will quickly destroy concentration on the job in hand.

The Judo outfit consists of twill jacket, belt, and trousers. The jacket is long and loose fitting, with wide sleeves reaching just below the elbows. It has no buttons, button-holes or pockets to cause injury, and is tied with a belt knotted in front, the color of the belt indicating the standard of proficiency reached by the wearer. The belt is eight feet long, goes twice round the body, and is secured by a special knot. Figures 1, 2, 3, 4 show the method of putting it on. Hold the middle of the belt in front of you and bind the ends round you in opposite directions, so that they cross at the back and return to meet again at the front (Figs. 1 & 2). Tie the first half of a reef knot, and pass one end under the two thicknesses of belt (Fig. 3). Now tie the second half of the reef knot (Fig. 4).

The trousers are supported by a tape which is permanently stitched at its middle to the back of the trouser band. The two ends are brought round to the front and passed through a loop in the trousers (Figs. 5, 6, 7). Now tie a bow as if you were knotting your shoelace (Fig. 8). Tie it round the trouser-loop and tuck the ends down inside the trousers to prevent them from being pulled undone (Fig. 9).

All judo is performed barefooted to avoid the bruises and contusions that would result from the wearing of boots and shoes. Except when actually on the mat, however, slippers must be worn to prevent the soles of the feet from picking up the dust of the floor and carrying it to the mat surface. Special judo slippers may be purchased, but ordinary fireside slippers from home are perfectly satisfactory.

Judo clothes feel somewhat strange the first time they are worn because they are cut essentially loose in order to give full freedom of movement. But they quickly become comfortable as one becomes accustomed to them.

Fig. 1   Fig. 2   Fig. 3

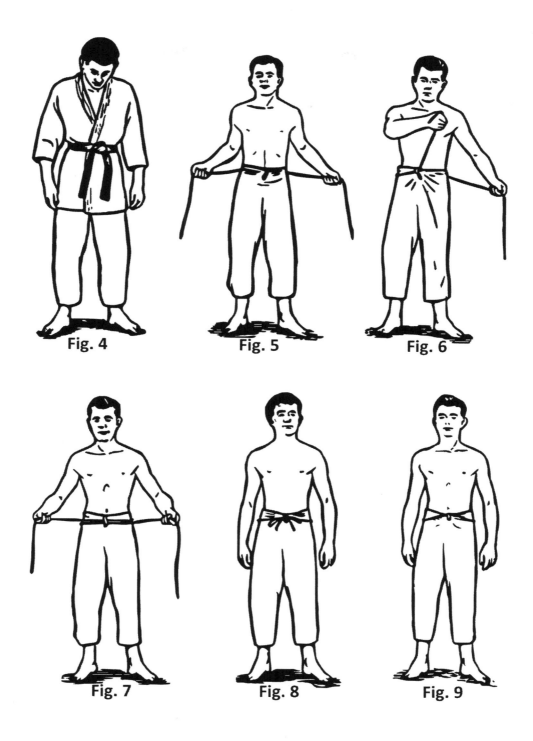

Fig. 4

Fig. 5

Fig. 6

Fig. 7

Fig. 8

Fig. 9

5

Grades and Grading

Grading is carried out by contest and by the demonstration of breakfalls, throws and groundwork according to the stage of proficiency reached by the individual candidate. Grading competitions are held quarterly; monthly in a few clubs. Marks are given for the following items, though not necessarily in this order of importance:

1. Marks for Contests won

2. Fighting Spirit

3. Style

4. Attacks attempted (whether successful or not)

5. Timing

6. Defence (to a lesser degree)

In the early days of instruction, it is quite common for the average pupil to progress from grade to grade at regular intervals of three months. This steady advance usually continues until 3rd Kyu (green belt). At this stage, however, the winning of contests begins to play an increasingly significant part in the judges' reckoning, and this factor has the effect of slowing down the rate of progress in the great majority of cases. It is not uncommon for Blue Belts and Brown Belts to wait for as long as two years for promotion to the next grade, though in my opinion this is much too long. Any judoka— as one who engages in judo is called—who is worth his salt and whose club enjoys the services of an experienced instructor should maintain a consistently high rate of progress. That so many of them do not is principally due to the fact that they cease to be receptive to instruction. They reach a stage when they begin to think they "know it all." Many a time have I listened to Blue and Brown Belts grumbling about their lack of promotion and attributing it to want of sympathy and perception in the grading officials responsible.

The raw novice starts with a red belt which is an unofficial color used for convenience to indicate that the wearer has yet to pass into the lowest official grade—the 6th Kyu. (Kyu means "grade" in Japanese.) In Europe the successive Kyu grades are as follows:

6th Kyu	White Belt
5th Kyu	Yellow Belt
4th Kyu	Orange Belt
3rd Kyu	Green Belt
2nd Kyu	Blue Belt
1st Kyu	Brown Belt

After the Kyus come the Dan or Master grades, in the first five of which the black belt is worn. From the sixth to twelfth Dan the colours are as shown in the table below.

6th to 8th Dan	Red-and-White Striped Belt
9th to 11th Dan	Red Belt
12th Dan	White Belt

The highest rank ever reached by other than a Japanese is 6th Dan, and by a Japanese, 10th Dan.

In the United States the same grades are used, but the colors of the belts differ as follows:

6th Kyu	White Belt
5th Kyu	
4th Kyu	Green Belt
3rd Kyu	Brown Belt
2nd Kyu	
1st Kyu	

Joining a Club

Maybe you will have no choice when it comes to joining a club, but if you live in the neighbourhood of a big city where there are two or more clubs open to you, you should make inquiries about the grades of the various instructors and their records as teachers. It is worth travelling a long way to obtain instruction from a Black Belt with a long record of successful teaching and who is not just a good "contest man."

The ideal introduction to judo is to join a class for beginners. There may be a waiting list, in which case be grateful and gladly wait your turn. The existence of a waiting list usually implies a thriving club whose instructional courses arc kept constantly full from personal recommendation. Visit the club before joining and watch the instruction taking place. All good clubs welcome visitors.

A Suggested Syllabus

While it is quite in order for the experienced judoka to practice the throws, locks and holds described in this book in any sequence that appeals to him most, the novice would be ill-advised to attempt to follow suit. His inclinations must be strictly governed by the degree of proficiency he has already reached, and by blind acceptance of the rule which lays down that the practice of judo must be essentially progressive from one stage to the next. Only harm can come from attempting too much too soon, and therefore some well-defined scale of progress is inescapable. But it must be flexible and adaptable to the individual. This last is most important and was the reason for the reluctance I expressed in the introductory chapter to this book to do more than suggest a framework on which progressive training may be based.

If the novice begins his judo career by joining a club—as he certainly should if there is one within reasonable range of his home—it is obviously much better that he should follow the planned program prescribed by his club than attempt to conform to a schedule of my recommendation. Not that there is likely to be any marked disparity between the two, because all such schedules are based on long experience of judo instruction, and where deviation occurs it will probably be only in matters of detail. The important consideration is the man himself. So much depends on the individual student, on his ability to absorb instruction, on his opportunities for practice and, indeed, on his suppleness of limb and his general physical fitness. These are unknown quantities which inevitably vary from man to man and make it unwise, if not impossible, to legislate in general terms. It is here that an experienced instructor, able to size up a man and advise him on his individual progress, can be of such inestimable value.

Nevertheless, lacking the advantage of an instructor on the spot, I realize that some guidance on the order in which the various falls and throws described in this book should be learned is essential. I have therefore drawn up a tentative schedule which, though it may be varied to suit different circumstances, can be safely accepted as a general guide to progressive instruction. In order to introduce some variety and added interest, I have broken down the schedule into groups of three or more. Each group should be reasonably well mastered before passing on to the next, and every training session should include some revision of what has already been learned, beginning always with the breakfalls. Randori (free practice) and contest practice should conclude each session after the fourth stage has been reached

As the pupil climbs the judo ladder, he will begin to see how quick changes of tactics can wrest success from failure. He will learn to combine throws, using one as a bluff to persuade his opponent to leave himself open to another. In groundwork he will learn to spot openings for armlocks when an opponent is struggling to escape from a hold-down, and how to develop a ground attack when an opponent is brought down but is not cleanly thrown.

These are all points which can be better learned from experience and intelligent observation than from the pages of a book. In this the club member has an immense advantage, and if he makes use of his opportunities of watching others perform, his own progress should advance by leaps and bounds.

STAGE	TECHNIQUES	STAGE	TECHNIQUES
I.	Backward Breakfall Sideways Breakfall Forward Breakfall	VII.	Shoulder Throw Using Jacket Reverse Scarf Hold Single Wing Choke
II.	Balance Hip Throw Scarf Hold	VIII.	Shoulder Drop Throw Naked Strangle Figure Four Arm Lock
III.	Hand Throw to Rear Major Outer Reaping Upper Four-Quarter Hold	IX.	Sweeping Loin Throw Knee Wheel Throw Straight Arm Lock from Astride Opponent
IV.	Hand Throw to Front Drawing Ankle Throw Broken Upper Four-Quarter Hold	X.	Sweeping Advancing Foot Throw Ankle Sweep Throw to Side Straight Arm Lock from Beneath Opponent
V.	Body Drop Throw Body Drop Throw to Side Normal Cross Strangle Adverse Cross Strangle Half Cross Strangle Straight Arm Lock Between Thighs	XI.	Leg Wheel Throw Arm Crush Forward Rolling Breakfall
VI.	Shoulder Throw Using Arm Side Four-Quarter Hold Cross Choke Straight Arm Lock from a Throw	XII.	Spring Hip Throw Rear Inner Ankle Throw Rear Outer Ankle Throw
		XIII.	Minor Inner Reaping Throw Major Inner Reaping Throw Stomach Throw

Continuity of Movement

All motion in judo is continuous, one movement merging imperceptibly into the next without break or pause, so that it is often difficult to determine precisely where one action ends and the next begins. Nevertheless, for the purposes of instruction it is necessary to break down this continuous movement into the diverse leg, arms and body movements which comprise the whole. This I have tried to do as smoothly and logically as possible. In the case of the breakfalls, which are usually the first judo techniques the beginner encounters, I have gone so far as to describe them by numbers. I hoped by this means to help the reader not only to grasp the essentials of each, but also to indicate to him a progressive method by which each may be learned.

I cannot stress too strongly, however, that the student should always try to visualize a particular technique as a continuous whole and not as a series of separate movements that must somehow be linked together. From the first movement to the last there is no break in the rhythm of a properly executed fall or throw.

I would also point out that all the falls, throws, holds, etc., can be made to the left or right, according to the direction in which your partner moves. For the purposes of this book I have described these movements to one side only, but the student should practice them to both sides, reading "left" for "right" and "right" for "left" when practicing to the opposite side to the one described.

Relaxation

Throughout the pages of this book you will constantly encounter references to "relaxation." This repetition is necessary because every technique in judo depends on the muscles of the body being comfortably relaxed. This does not mean that they are slack and sloppy, unable to do their appointed work; it means they are loose and responsive, free from unwanted tension, ready to give but never to break.

The simple little experiment of forcefully throwing to the ground two sticks illustrates how important is relaxation to the success of any breakfall. If one of the sticks is dry and brittle it will readily snap in two under the stress of impact; if the other is green and pliable it will bend instead of breaking and will suffer no damage. The same principle applies to the limbs of the body—relaxed, they will give to the impact of the fall; tense, they will resist it and suffer hurt in consequence.

Balance

The fundamental basis of all judo is to break your opponent's balance while preserving your own. Insecure balance comes from poor relaxation and careless movement. Take the wonderfully relaxed movements of the domestic cat as an example; notice how easy and graceful they are, note the lazy suppleness of the spine, and how the toes always point straight to the front. That is how the judoka should move—loose, poised, knees slightly bent, feet pointing directly along the line of advance, or as near directly as you can manage.

Figure 10 shows the student advancing his left foot; the toes of this foot point directly along his line of advance. Figure 11 shows the same movement with the right foot.

Figure 12 shows student stepping to the left. In this case the left foot is turned as far to the left as can be managed in comfort. Don't overdo this to the extent that it feels strained and awkward—the leg must remain relaxed. Figure 13 shows the same movement to the right.

Fig. 10   **Fig. 11**   **Fig. 12**

The positioning of the feet is all-important to balance, especially when you come to learn the throws. The toes of the foot on which your weight and balance are poised at the moment that the throw is made must always point in the direction in which you intend you r opponent to fall. The same rule applies to the knee on which weight and balance are centered at any time—it must be directly over the toes and kept there throughout (Figs. 14 & 15). Similarly, when stepping forward, the shoulder corresponding to the leg moved must be over the knee so that toes, knee and shoulder are in a vertical line (Fig. 16). Figure 17 shows the wrong position, with weight on back foot.

It is equally important to keep the knee perpendicularly over the toes in making a step to the side. In Figure 18 the student has carried his right foot to the right and has kept his right knee and shoulder over it. He is well balanced. In Figure 19 he has allowed his right knee and shoulder to over- run his toes; in this position he is open to a throw to his right, and requires only a slight push to make him fall. This is one of the commonest faults in Judo.

Fig. 13   **Fig. 14**   **Fig. 15**   **Fig. 16**

Fig. 17   **Fig. 18**   **Fig. 19**

The Position of the Hands

When two contestants square up to each other, the customary hold is for each to grip the left lapel of the other with his right hand at a height approximately level with his own chest. The two left hands grasp ·the underside of the opponent's right sleeve just below the elbow. (See Fig. 71.)

Although these holds will necessarily change in the course of many of the techniques described, long practice has shown them to be the most efficient for the majority of purposes, and they should be adopted in every case by beginners for the opening maneuvers.

In all throws it is essential to maintain throughout your hold on your opponent's jacket. In throws to the left, it is the left hand which holds on; to the right, the right hand. It may look spectacular when an opponent goes sailing through the air to strike the mat some feet away, but it is bad policy because once you let go of an opponent you lose control of his movements, and if the throw is not clean enough to win you the point outright, you are right back where you started. Retain contact with him, however, and the advantage remains with you, enabling you instantly to renew the attack with an arm-lock or hold-down.

Furthermore, by holding on—and this is particularly important in practice bouts—you are able to break the full force of your opponent' s fall by taking some of his weight just before he strikes the mat.

Movement of the Legs, Hips and Body

The successful execution of even the simplest judo exercise is the result of coordinated movement, in which one set of muscles works in conjunction with other sets of muscles to produce a result that no one set of muscles could achieve on its own. If, for instance, you used only your arms to pull your opponent towards you (Fig. 20), ignoring the rest of your body, comparatively little power would be transmitted to him. The same would be true if you used only the shoulder muscles (Fig. 21).

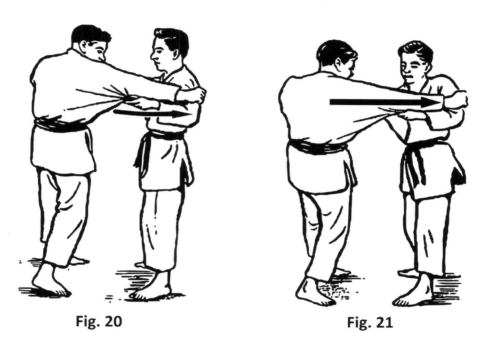

Fig. 20   **Fig. 21**

Now take up the correct judo position (Fig. 22), knees slightly bent, hands grasping opponent's jacket. Begin a turning movement to your left by withdrawing your left hip and swinging your left leg away from your opponent (Fig. 23). As you do so, curve your body slightly forward—the position of maximum strength—and pull with your left arm and push with the right in the same arc as that taken by the withdrawing hip (Figs. 24 & 25). In other words, the whole body moves and works in coordination to produce the maximum result. (Note also how the toes of the thrower's right foot are turned in the direction in which opponent will fall.)

The withdrawal of the hip is the key to the movement. Thus, when you read, or are told by an instructor, to "step back with your left foot," what is really meant is "withdraw your left hip and your leg and body must go with it." The hip movement also has another important function in that it enables you to make all movements in circles.

15

Figure 25 shows the different circular movements involved in breaking an opponent's balance to his right front.

Fig. 22

Fig. 23

Fig. 24

Fig. 25

A wheel spinning horizontally on its axle provides a good illustration of the forces at work (Fig. 26). The hub "A" controls the movement of the wheel. When the wheel is spinning, the hub turns much less fast than the outer rim "B" because it has less far to travel. In judo the thrower is at "A", his victim at "B". Consequently, the thrower moves slowly and under control while the victim is whirled round fast, and the faster he goes the more likely he is to lose control of his own movements. Thus, the man at "A" has a considerable advantage which he must maintain at all costs. Should he step from his central point—by moving the foot on which he proposes to make his throw, for instance—he will break the rhythm of his own turning motion, thereby giving his opponent the opportunity to turn the tables by placing himself at the hub of the wheel.

Circular movement operates throughout judo on a wide variety of planes as may be seen from a close study of the text and sketches in this book.

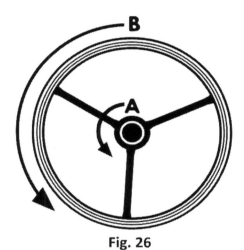

Fig. 26

Throws to Opponent's Front

For all practical purposes, judo throws can be divided into two categories—those to the opponent's front and those to his rear. There are, of course, many others to the left and right, but these are only variations of the two main categories and have no place in a book of the scope of the present one. The beginner need not worry his head about them for some time to come.

Throws to an opponent's front are usually made against an opponent who, (I) adopting an upright stance, advances on you, or (II) adopting an upright stance and standing still, is thrusting at you preparatory to advancing. A crouching opponent is normally thrown to the rear whichever way he is moving, though such throws as the Inner Thigh are exceptions to this rule. In order to throw your opponent to his front you must first turn away from him. You therefore place yourself in a vulnerable position unless you have effectively broken his balance and can continue to keep him off balance throughout. The principal points to remember are:

1. Do not attack without first breaking opponent's balance—Unless he breaks it for you.

2. Keep him off balance throughout the throw.

3. Maintain your own balance throughout the throw.

Although these rules also apply to rear throws, they are more important in forward throws because of your vulnerability to counter measures.

Throws to Opponent's Rear

The basic points to remember when executing throws to the rear are as follows:

1. Opponent must be pinned immobile to the mat with his weight on his heels at the outset of the attack. All is lost if you allow him to retreat before your advance (Fig. 27).

2. Your body must be arched forward as you step in to break his balance to the rear and bring your weight to bear on him (Fig. 28).

3. Your forward foot—that is, the foot on which you stand to make the throw—must be level with opponent's retreating foot—preferably even beyond it (Fig. 29).

4. The full drive of your hands and arms must be directly downward towards the mat (Fig. 30)—never backwards towards your opponent's rear.

Fig. 27

Fig. 28

Fig. 29

Fig. 30

The Ceremonial Bow

(Standing: *Tachirei* / **Kneeling:** *Zarei*)

At one time all practice bouts, known as randori, commenced and ended with the ceremonial bow. In this, the contestants take their places on the mat, sitting on their heels and facing each other about six feet apart (Fig. 31). When both are ready, they place their hands on the mat just in front of their knees and incline their bodies forward, showing the tops of their heads to each other (Fig. 32).

Although the ceremonial bow is still observed in many clubs, the less formal bow from the hips (Fig. 33) is rapidly becoming more common and is acceptable in most clubs on all but the most ceremonial occasions.

Fig. 31

Fig. 32

Fig. 33

CHAPTER III
The Breakfalls

How To Fall (Ukemi)

The first essential on taking up judo is to learn to fall correctly. Until you can do so, you will not be able to join in at throwing practice, because participation in throwing practice implies your being thrown in return by another member of your class.

Therefore, start every session with breakfall practice, devoting ten minutes to it on each occasion. Take your time over each type of fall, and make quite sure you have mastered the simpler movements before passing to the more difficult. A badly executed fall due to faulty technique is both painful and destructive of confidence, and without confidence it is impossible to improve. You may even be unaware of having lost your confidence, but a good instructor will see it; so don't hesitate to ask the instructor to watch you at regular intervals. In spite of the importance of mastering correct falling, ten-minute practice spells are quite sufficient while you are still in the novice class. Enthusiasm is all very well, but if you overdo it you will finish each session with sore muscles and an aching head.

All falls are taken with the body curled up and relaxed, the arms, acting as shock-absorbers, striking the mat momentarily before the impact of the body. Experienced judoka also use their feet to break a fall, but beginners should concentrate on the arms alone because use of the feet in breaking a fall makes relaxation more difficult. It also has the effect of straightening the body, thus endangering the spine to injury if not properly executed. The body is curled up so that the' spine, head, hips, knees and other vulnerable points are kept clear of the ground and the impetus of the fall is expended in a harmless roll. The whole length of the arms from fingertips to shoulders strikes the mat simultaneously as one piece.

The Backward Breakfall

You are unlikely to have to perform this breakfall in contests early in your judo career because it is mostly used to counter advanced throws such as you are not likely to meet as a novice. Furthermore, it is not a fall to be recommended to beginners because, inexpertly executed, it can be dangerous. Despite this, it is usually the first breakfall to be learned because it includes all the basic principles in an easily recognized form and is at the same time an admirable judo exercise.

Stage I—Squat on your heels with your · head tucked well in so that you are looking down at your belt, your arms held loosely in front of you (Fig. 34). Now gently roll over on to your back until loss of momentum stops further movement (Fig. 35). It does not matter how far you roll; you may even go completely over, though it is unlikely that you will. Repeat this exercise until you can do it with- out any sign of muscular tension. If in rolling backwards you find that further movement is stopped by your head or shoulders, it is because your body is not fully curled up due to insufficient relaxation.

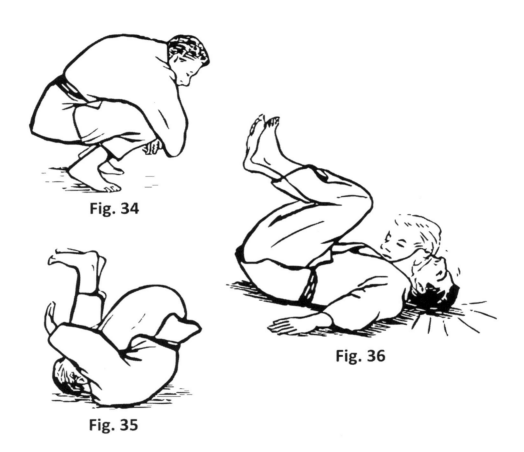

Fig. 34

Fig. 35

Fig. 36

When this happens it will not be long before you develop a headache. Figure 36 shows this unrelaxed position with the correct position superimposed. A glance at the wrong position suggests how painful would be the effect of a heavy fall.

Stage 2—Lie on your back in a curled-up position so that your head and legs are well up and your arms are extended on the mat, palms of the hands down, at an angle of about 45° to your body (Fig. 37). This is the position in which you take a fall to the rear. Now raise your arms above your head (Fig. 38) and, keeping them relaxed, beat them downwards on to the mat. In doing this aim your fingertips at the corners of the room—this helps to get the correct angle between arms and body—and don't be afraid to beat down hard; the whole essence of this action lies in the power with which your arms strike the mat. Provided that your arms are relaxed and you are practicing on a proper judo mat or other suitably soft surface, you will come to no harm. When watching advanced judoka perform this breakfall you may think that their arms are tense and rigid at the moment of impact. Don't be deceived by this; despite appearances, their arms are perfectly relaxed.

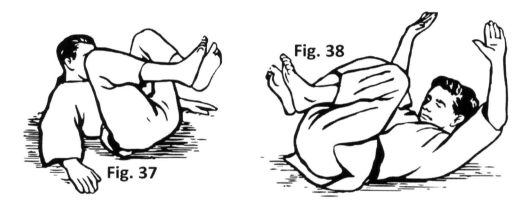

Fig. 37

Fig. 38

Even the most flexible of objects can appear to be unbending under certain circumstances, as you can demonstrate for yourself with a short length of rubber hose. Held in the hand the hose is so pliable that it bends double under its own weight (Fig. 39); but if it is suddenly whipped up and then downwards it straightens out like a rod and gives the erroneous impression of being quite stiff as it strikes the ground (Fig. 40). The same principle applies to your arms in this and in every other judo fall.

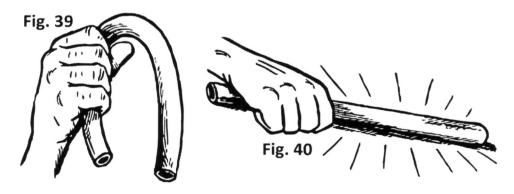

Fig. 39

Fig. 40

Stage 3—When Stage 2 is working to your satisfaction, the next step is one of timing. Instead of beating your arms to the mat from the lying position, you must learn to do so as you roll backwards from the squatting position, beating the mat momentarily before your body makes contact. It is this split-second timing that produces the "shock-

Fig. 41

absorber" effect. Adopt position shown in Figure 41—squatting, with arms outstretched. Roll over backwards and bring the arm action into play—from shoulder to fingertip in a vigorous downward beat a fraction of a second before the body lands. It will help your timing if you begin the downward beat at the same moment as you begin to roll backwards.

Stage 4—This is the final stage. All that now remains is to perfect the fall at steadily increasing heights from the ground until you can do it from the standing position. Begin by straightening your knees a little from the original squatting position before you roll back. As you progress, go on straightening them until you can confidently hurl yourself backwards when standing upright, or nearly upright (Fig. 42), breaking your fall harmlessly with your arms. Do not be in too great a hurry to reach this advanced stage. Confidence comes with practice, but do not make practice sessions too long—ten minutes on any one technique is quite sufficient. And don't be discouraged if progress seems slow; you can look forward to several months of regular practice before you can perform this fall from a standing position even moderately well.

Fig. 42

The Breakfall Sideways (Yoko Ukemi)

This is the most common fall in judo; indeed, with the possible exception of the Forward Rolling Fall to a stomach throw, it is practically the only fall a beginner is likely to encounter.

Fig. 43

Stage 1—Lie on your back with the body curled up, chin tucked in, and knees drawn up. Now roll to your right, at the same time beating down on the mat with your right arm so that the whole arm from shoulder to fingertips strikes the mat at the same instant (Fig. 43). The angle that the arm makes with the body must not greatly exceed 45° because, owing to the construction of the shoulder joint, a greater angle prohibits free movement and, with loss of freedom, tension creeps in. Unless the arm is completely relaxed, bruising of the elbow and shoulder will result. Throughout this exercise the left arm should be lying loosely across the body wherever it is most comfortable.

After several practice beats to the right, roll over to your left side and beat with your left arm. It is necessary to be equally proficient on both wings, although in combat it is more often to the left that you have to breakfall. This is because most people, being right-handed, have a tendency to throw to their left.

Stage 2—When you can confidently perform Stage I to the right and left, you can combine the two in an excellent exercise. Beat first to your right (Fig. 44) and, as your arm rebounds from the mat, roll over to your other side and beat to the left (Figs. 45 & 46). Then roll back to the right and repeat until you begin to tire. Not only is this a first-class exercise for getting the body supple but, more important, it brings you automatically into the correct position of the breakfall and gives you the "feel" of what you are trying to do. In combat your disengaged arm will either be held by your opponent or itself will be grasping opponent's belt or clothing (Fig. 53).

Stage 3—All that now remains is to practice the fall from progressively greater heights from the ground. Begin in the squatting position (Fig. 47) and roll to your right. Just before your body touches the mat, breakfall with your right arm. Repeat the motion to the left. At this stage you may find that your head has a tendency to snap backwards as the breakfall is made. This is a sure sign that your chin is not tucked sufficiently close in to your chest.

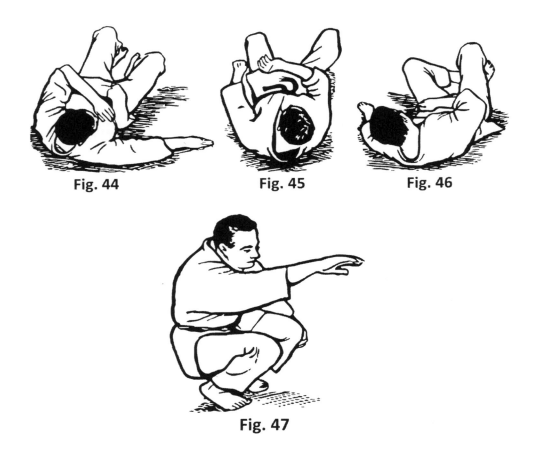

Fig. 44   **Fig. 45**   **Fig. 46**

Fig. 47

Gradually increase the height of the fall by progressively straightening your knees. As you get higher it is easier to make the fall if you initiate the movement by swinging the leg on the side you propose to fall forward and across the other leg.

Figure 48 shows an initial sideways movement of the right leg across the left preparatory to breakfalling to the right. As the right leg crosses the left you will begin to lose your balance and start falling to the right (Fig. 49); as you do so raise your right arm in readiness for the down beat of the breakfall. Continue this exercise until you can breakfall sideways to both sides from the erect position.

Fig. 48   **Fig. 49**

Stage 4—The final stage is to execute this breakfall in partnership with another student. Stand sideways to him and grip his belt with your right hand while he, standing firmly with feet apart, grasps your right sleeve at the elbow with his left hand. Your right foot should be a short pace in advance of your left foot and about level with your opponent's right foot (Fig. 50).

Now swing your left leg vigorously from the hip (Fig. 51), allowing the impetus of it to swing your right foot off the mat to follow in the same upward arc. Breakfall sideways to your left (Fig. 52). Your partner gripping your sleeve will help to break the full force of your fall and you will assist by taking some of your weight on his belt (Fig. 53). This combined exercise comes as near to conveying the sensation of being thrown as one can get without actually taking a throw. With practice you soon will be able to take considerable falls of this kind with complete confidence.

Note that when practicing this fall with a partner the movement of the swinging leg is forwards and upwards; when practicing it on your own (as in Stage 3) the movement of the swinging leg is sideways across the body. This is because when working with a partner your grip on his belt and his hold on your sleeve bring you into the correct breakfall position. Working alone, you must fall sideways to avoid landing flat on your back.

Fig. 50

Fig. 51

Fig. 52

Fig. 53

Instructors Ted Cribben and E. Wilkin have one of the best methods I know for introducing beginners to breakfalls. The pupil holds the instructor's left lapel while the instructor places his right arm under the pupil's right leg and takes hold of the front of the pupil's belt. With his left hand the instructor grasps the back of the pupil's jacket (Fig. 54). The instructor then swings the pupil off the mat forwards and upwards (Fig. 55), supporting him as he falls (Fig. 56).

Fig. 54

Fig. 55

Fig. 56

The Breakfall Forward (Koho Ukemi)

This is another breakfall which does not often occur in combat but with which every judoka must be familiar. It is used to meet a throw to the front such as would be dangerous if the victim had no knowledge of how to deal with it. The Breakfall Forward is widely reckoned to be one of the most difficult falls in judo, and the student who has difficulty in learning it would be well advised to leave it alone—at least in its final stage—until he has had more experience and practice in judo generally.

The object of the fall is to protect the knees, body and head from violent contact with the ground, and it differs in execution from other falls in that the fall is broken by toes and forearms only (Fig. 60).

Fig. 57

Stage 1—Kneel down, sitting on your heels, with the hands raised (Fig. 57). Now pivot forward on your knees to beat the mat with the forearms and palms of the hands (Fig. 58). This should present no great difficulty. The next step is to do the same thing from the upright kneeling position and this, too, calls for no very great accomplishment. The principal difficulty lies in the second stage.

Fig. 58

Stage 2—You now have to take the fall from the standing position. Stand upright and allow yourself to tip forward slowly as in Figure 59. Notice the curve of the body and how its whole weight is taken first on the toes, the fall being broken by the full extent of the hands and forearms (Fig. 60). The final goal of this exercise is achieved when you can successfully make this fall after launching yourself into the air from a running jump. It is an accomplishment that takes much time and practice.

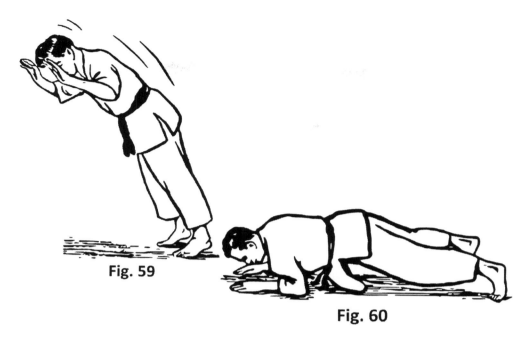

Fig. 59

Fig. 60

The Forward Rolling Breakfall (Chugaeri)

This fall is made in response to a Stomach Throw or similar form of attack and should not be attempted by the novice. In early practice it is important to perform it slowly and with careful attention, as mistakes can be painful. The essential points to remember are to keep your head well tucked into your chest as you roll forward, and to remain completely relaxed throughout.

Stage 1—Take up position shown in Figure 60, taking care that the fingers of the hands point inwards towards each other so that the wrists are not bent backwards as you go over. The illustration shows the palms of the hands down on mat. I prefer this position although some instructors recommend that the little finger edge of the hand only should be in contact with the mat. Either position is correct and you may use whichever you prefer. From the position shown in Figure 61 push off with your right foot and roll on to the mat over your right arm and shoulder (Figs. 62 & 63). If your head is tucked in as it should be it will not touch the ground. Note that the roll is always made either to one side or the other; it is never directly forward like a tumbler's roll. Roll diagonally right over your right arm, diagonally left over your left arm. Unless you roll diagonally you cannot beat with the other arm, and will probably land on your back with a thump.

In your early attempts confine yourself to rolling over; but as you get more proficient bring the other arm into play to beat the mat momentarily before the body strikes (Fig. 64). Contact with the mat should be made first by the supporting arm then, just as the back is about to touch, by the other arm beating in breakfall.

31

Fig. 61

Fig. 62

Fig. 63

Fig. 64

As you gain in confidence and your falls become more ambitious, you must remember to keep the supporting arm straight—though not rigid. Should it collapse you will land on your head or neck. It helps at this advanced stage if, when pushing off at the start of the roll, you thrust forward and slightly upward in order to "spread" the fall. The more you spread it by continuing the forward roll, the less likely you are to collapse on the fall and land flat on your back.

Stage 2—The next requirement is to perform this breakfall while on the move. Begin by taking no more than a single pace forward and, reaching forward and down with right or left hand, roll over it to the appropriate side. With practice you will be able to do it at the run and from either side. In combat the supporting hand plays no part; because of the impetus given to your roll by your opponent, no part of your body touches the mat until your beating arm has absorbed much of the shock.

In the first stage (Fig. 61) the left hand need not be placed on the ground, but many students find it helps to do so in their early attempts.

CHAPTER IV
The Ankle Throws Ankle Throws and Throws to Opponent's Rear

These are the throws in which you attack your opponent's ankle. They range in difficulty from the comparatively simple Drawing Ankle Throw to the complex Inner Reaping and Rear Ankle Throws. Although I have included descriptions of them all in this chapter, common sense and discretion must be exercised as to the order in which they are learnt, and for guidance on this point I would refer you to the recommended schedule on page 22. All the throws described may be made with either foot, depending on which way your opponent moves. I have described them to one side only as the reader should have no difficulty in applying the instructions to the other side.

The essence of all ankle throws is to push your opponent's foot across the mat surface—not to lift it off the mat (see direction of arrow in Figure 65). This is most important because, however well you perform the rest of the throw, if you attempt to lift with your throwing foot your opponent has only to lift his attacked foot to step clear (Fig. 66). Another important point to remember is that your disengaged foot—that is, the foot which is not attacking your opponent's ankle—must point in the direction in which you intend your opponent to fall. Unless it is so pointing, you will not be able to move sufficiently nimbly to make the throw.

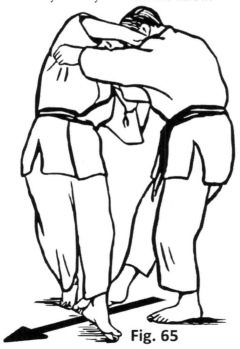

Fig. 65

Fig. 66

33

The Drawing Ankle Throw (Tsuri Komiashi)

Neat execution of this throw requires good balance and timing. You and opponent are facing each other, each holding jacket with the normal lapel and sleeve hold (Fig. 71). Opponent steps forward with his right foot and just as his weight comes on to it, you attack with your left foot. Good timing is necessary here in order to take advantage of his forward motion to pull him still farther forward while checking further movement of his right foot.

Although in theory this is not a difficult throw to perform moderately well, it is not an easy one to put into execution in the course of a contest against an agile opponent unless it has been truly mastered. For this reason, it is worthy of persistent practice.

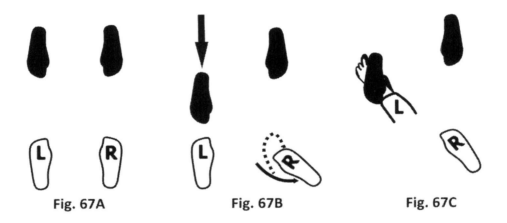

Fig. 67A   **Fig. 67B**   **Fig. 67C**

As your opponent comes forward on his right foot, perhaps pushing you with his right hand, assist his forward movement by drawing him on with your left hand, turning to the left on the ball of your right foot as you do so (Fig. 67B), and bending your right knee at the same time. Pivot to the left as far as you can, withdrawing your left. hip clear so that your body does not impede his forward movement. Push with your right hand and pull with your left in the same arc as followed by your left hip in withdrawing.

Continue to draw him on, and place the sole of your left foot at the base of his right shin to prevent his advancing farther and so recovering his balance (Figs. 67C & 68).

Continue to withdraw your left hip and keep pulling with your left hand and pushing with the right in a circular turning motion until he is thrown to the mat over your left foot (Fig. 69). Do not try to root his foot to any particular part of the mat. To do so, you would have to push forward with your own foot and this would prevent you from swinging your hip clear. The secret is to keep drawing him on to your foot by steadily taking your hip back. Success lies in the steady pull and push of the left and right arms and in keeping your own body clear of his forward advance. As you pivot on the ball of your right foot, withdraw your left hip as far as possible and push with your right hand in the same turning movement. This will ensure that your opponent continues to come forward in the precise direction he originally moved in, and keeps coming forward until he falls.

Fig. 68   **Fig. 69**

SWEEPING ANKLE THROWS

Sweeping the Advancing Foot (Deashiharai)

Fig. 70

This is one of the easiest throws to understand in theory, but a difficult one to perfect because of its dependence on timing. The object is to sweep your opponent's leg from beneath him at the precise moment that he transfers his weight to it. As you sweep his leg away with your foot, your body and arms throw him downwards to the mat just where his supporting leg should have been (Fig. 70).

Take up the normal hold on your opponent's jacket. The throw becomes possible immediately your opponent steps forward with either leg—in the present example, his right leg (Fig. 71).

Fig. 71

*When two contestants square up to each other, the customary hold
is for each to grip the left lapel of the other with his right hand at a
height approximately level with his own chest. The two left hands
grasp the underside of the opponents' right sleeves just below the elbow.*

Your opponent comes forward and you place the sole of your left foot at the base of his right shin just as he brings his weight upon it (Figs. 72A & 73). Sweep his leg from under him, inclining your body to the left as you sweep so that it maintains a straight line with your sweeping leg (Fig. 75). Your left hand pulls him downwards in a circular motion while your right hand lifts upwards in completion of the same circle (Figs. 74 & 75).

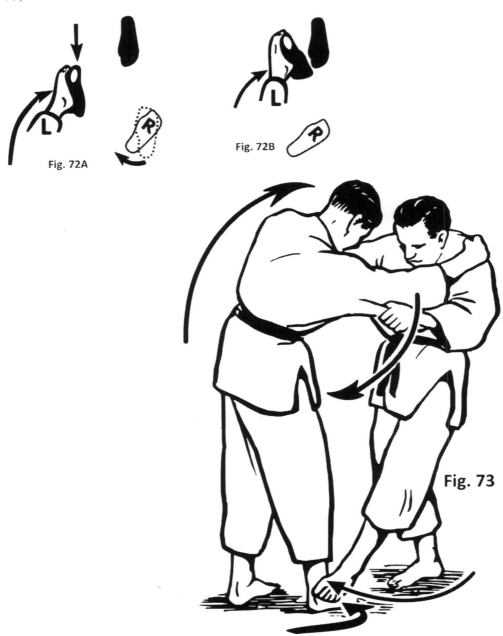

Fig. 72A

Fig. 72B

Fig. 73

Fig. 74

Fig. 75

Fig. 76

Fig. 77

In sweeping his leg to the right you should attempt to make it pass as close as possible to his supporting leg (Fig.76); it does not matter if you misjudge this and sweep it so close that his two legs become locked together (Figs. 72B & 77). Indeed, it often helps. It also helps if you turn your own right foot slightly to the right as you sweep. The secret of success in this throw is to overcome the natural tendency to lift upwards with your attacking foot. The thrust of your sweep must be horizontally across the mat's surface.

Ankle Sweep to the Side (Okuri-Ashi-Harai)

This throw differs from other ankle throws in that the attacker follows his opponent's movement instead of initiating the attack or at least persuading his opponent to move in a desired direction. It is also one of the few throws in judo which can be made when an opponent is moving to the side. Figure 78A shows an opponent moving to his left; your object is to sweep away his right foot in the instant he takes it from the mat in order to complete his step to the left (Fig. 78B). Timing is of particular importance in this throw because if your attack is mistimed your opponent will be able to step clear or will remain immovable when you sweep. In Figure 78A the opponent sidesteps to his left and you follow to your right. As he completes this step, use your arms to break his balance. Your left arm pushes him downwards and to his left, and your right pushes him upwards and to his right (Fig. 79). At the same time sweep his right foot away from beneath him with the sole of your left foot (Figs. 78B & 80). In doing so, keep your left leg and the left side of your body in a straight line so that your arms do not move individually but as part of a whole-body movement. For example, as the left foot sweeps along the mat, the left hip dips and the left. hand and arm circle to your right. Correspondingly, your right arm comes up and over to your left. Try this for yourself, as shown in Figure 75. This rotary movement is true of all judo movements but is particularly important in this throw.

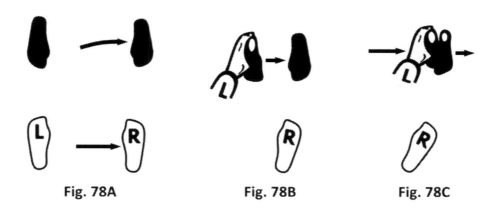

Fig. 78A   Fig. 78B   Fig. 78C

Fig. 79   Fig. 80

The sweep may be made so that opponent's foot is swept across the mat, passing in front of his other (Fig. 81); or it may be made so that his foot is swept hard up against the other (Fig. 78c). If your timing and technique are good, the latter is the more effective as in this case both his feet are swept from the mat (Fig. 80).

The points to watch in executing this throw are:

1. To time your attack so that you sweep his foot just as it is taken from, or replaced on, the mat. If you are early, it will still be firmly rooted to the ground; if you are late, his balance will be secure and you will be unable to upset him.

2. To bear opponent downwards over the spot where his right foot would have been (Fig. 80). Remember the sweeping motion must be low and close to the mat. Any upward thrust of your foot will nullify the advantage you have gained.

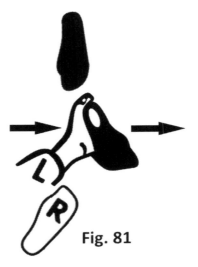

Fig. 81

42

THROWS TO OPPONENT'S REAR

The Minor Outer Reaping (Kosotogari)

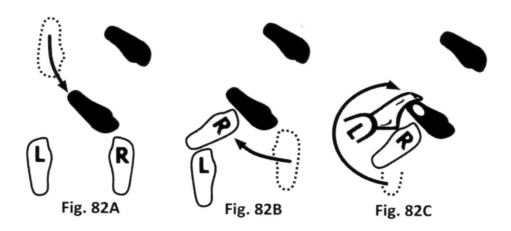

Fig. 82A   **Fig. 82B**   **Fig. 82C**

This is in many ways the easiest of the Ankle Throws once you have maneuvered your opponent so that he is standing sideways-on to you. Alternatively, he may invite this form of attack by himself turning sideways-on to you to avoid some other type of throw or to get himself into position for an attack of his own (Fig. 83). Figure 82A shows how opponent has stepped forward half-left with his right foot.

Immediately he reaches this position, step in with your right foot, placing it close against his right foot. Turn on your right foot as far as you can to the right (Fig. 82B). Simultaneously, curve your body forward and pin him securely on his heels by bearing down with your hands. In this action your left hand drives him directly downwards; your right hand, downwards and backwards. Your right wrist is curved down, back of the hand uppermost, and exerts a downward and backward circular movement against his shoulder (Fig. 84). This will break his balance to his rear. Hold him in this position and bring the sole of your left foot against the back of his right heel, pushing it in the direction in which his toes are pointing (Figs. 82C & 85). The action of your hands and body bearing downward, combining with the thrust of your left foot against his right heel, will throw him to his back (Fig. 86). Remember, it is essential to curve your body forward in order to bring its full power into action. If you remain upright you can only apply the strength of your arms, and this may not be sufficient to complete the throw.

Fig. 83
Opponent becomes vulnerable to a Rear Inner Ankle Throw when he turns sideways-on to you

Fig. 84
Your right wrist is curved down, back of the hand uppermost, and exerts a downward and backward movement against opponent's left shoulder.

Fig. 85   **Fig. 86**

The Rear Outer Ankle Throw (Kohosoto-Gari)

The opportunity for this attack occurs when your opponent has turned sideways to you (Figs. 87 & 88).

Step in with your right foot, placing it close up to your opponent's right heel and turning it as far as possible to the right (Fig. 89). Simultaneously, break opponent's balance to the rear by arching your body forward, and pin him down on his heels by transmitting your weight to him through your hands. Your left hand, grasping his right sleeve, pulls vertically downward; and your right hand, with wrist well bent so that the knuckles point to the floor, pushes downward against his shoulder (Fig. 90).

Your left hand grasps his right sleeve and pulls vertically downward. Your right hand, with wrist bent so that the knuckles point to the floor, exerts a downward thrust against his shoulder.

Fig. 87

Fig. 88

Fig. 89

Fig. 90

The left arm may be bent at the elbow as shown in Figure 90, but in my opinion a more effective result is obtained by straightening the arm at the elbow so that the knuckles of your left hand point directly to the ground (Fig. 29).

To complete the throw, place the sole of your left foot behind his left heel and thrust it along the mat in the direction his toes are pointing in (Fig. 91).

Fig. 91

The Minor Inner Reaping (Kouchi-Gari)

This is perhaps the most difficult of all ankle throws and throws to the rear. It is made as opponent steps to the rear with his left foot. As he retreats, advance your right foot, turning on it to the right (Fig. 92A). Arch your body forward and slightly bend your right knee. Bear him back on to his heels and press him down towards the mat. While your left hand drives vertically down, your right presses down against his collarbone (Figs. 93 and 94).

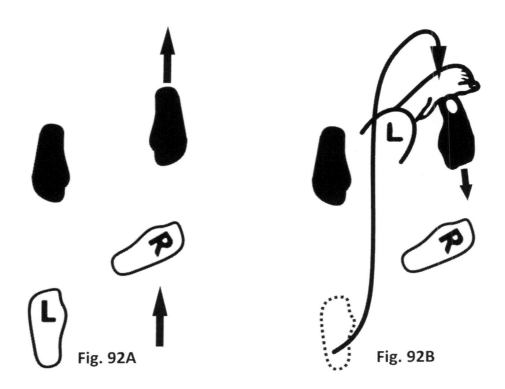

Fig. 92A   **Fig. 92B**

In this position opponent should be firmly anchored on his heels and leaning over backwards. Holding him there, slide your left foot between his legs so that the sole of your foot attacks the back of his left heel (Figs. 92B & 94). Now attempt to drag his left foot towards you, while maintaining the downward thrust of your arms and body. Even though you do not succeed in shifting his foot, your opponent will be thrown if you have succeeded in breaking his balance.

When the victim falls there is a tendency for the attacker to fall on top of him. This must be avoided whenever possible, as injury to one or both may result.

Bear him back on to his heels and press him down towards the mat. Slide your left foot between his legs so that the sole of your foot attacks the back of his left heel.

Fig. 93

Bear him back on to his heels and press him down towards the mat.

Fig. 94

Slide your left foot between his legs so that the sole of your foot attacks the back of his left heel.

The Major Outer Reaping (Osoto-Gari)

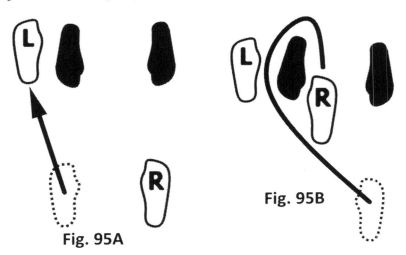

Fig. 95A

Fig. 95B

This throw is really no more than a continuation of the Hand Throw to the Rear, and is used against an opponent who is moving backwards or whose balance has moved backwards. In Figure 95A, your opponent is firmly planted on the mat with his weight just back of dead center. You step forward with your left foot, bringing it to the ground outside his right foot, if possible just beyond it. In taking this step, curve your body forward and drive him vertically downwards with your hands, breaking his balance to his rear (Fig. 96). Now bring your right leg forward so that it passes outside and beyond his right leg and then swings back to the position between his legs shown in Figure 95B. (See also Fig. 97.) The back of your right thigh is now firmly locked against the back of his right thigh as you thrust backwards from the hip in the direction shown in Figure 98. Keep bearing him vertically downwards to the mat.

Fig. 96

Fig. 97
Your right foot passes outside his right foot and swings back to the position shown in Fig. 95B.

Fig. 98
Keep bearing him vertically downwards to the mat.

The resultant fall is invariably heavy because, having concentrated most of your combined weights on to his right leg, you remove this support from under him. Practice should therefore be conducted with care and consideration of the other man.

Fig. 99A **Fig. 99B**

Occasionally it occurs that an opponent is very stubborn and successfully resists your attempts to thrust his leg from under him. When this happens, you can sometimes bring about his downfall by turning half-left (Figs. 99A and B & 100) as you make your sweep. This practice, however, cannot be recommended as a habit because it is really a confession of failure, and wide-awake opponents will soon spot the weakness and use it to their advantage.

Fig. 100

The Major Inner Reaping (Ouchi-Gari)

This is a leg throw and, although similar in principle to the Minor Inner Reaping, is much easier to perform. It is used when an opponent is standing in a defensive posture with feet level, or when he is standing with one leg advanced and balanced on it (Fig. 102). With your opponent thus on the defensive, step in with your left foot (Fig.101A). Your knee should be slightly bent, your body curving forward. Pin him to the mat with your hands to prevent him from retreating before your attack.

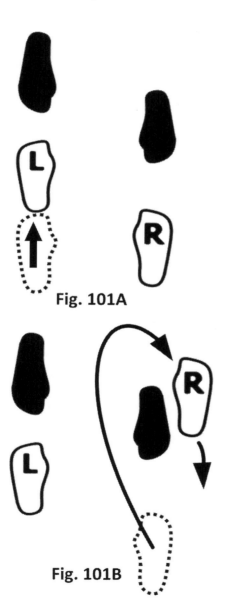

Fig. 101A

Fig. 101B

Drive directly downwards with your left hand, and with bent right wrist push backwards and downwards against his collarbone. Maintaining this pressure, swing your right leg between his legs and hook it round the back of his left leg (Figs. 101B & 102). Draw his leg back towards you by steady pressure of your hip (Fig. 103). If this pressure does not come from the hip, the movement will lose its effect, being upward instead of straight back.

55

Fig. 102

Fig. 103

General Notes on Throws to the Rear

All the rear throws are made against an opponent who is on the defensive, with knees bent. More occasionally they are made against an opponent retreating to his rear. No throw to the opponent's rear can succeed if you let him step away as you step in to attack; it is essential that you pin him to the mat with his balance broken over his heels. To do this you must curve your body forward as you step in and use you r hands and arms correctly in order to pin him down. The most common cause of failure is to be found in the wrong use of the right hand. The action of this hand, with wrist well bent, must be a backward and downward thrust against the collarbone.

CHAPTER V
Hand Throws

The proficient performance of Hand Throws is no easy accomplishment and is beyond the capability of the beginner. Nevertheless, instruction in these throws invariably forms a part of the beginner's curriculum because the movements on which they depend are basic movements throughout judo. Hand Throws require a well-developed sense of timing and, unlike some other throws, a faulty technique cannot be masked by the advantage of greater physical strength. In this book I have contented myself with the description of two throws only one to the front and one to the rear.

The novice is advised to view these throws strictly as exercises. He is unlikely to bring one off successfully in randori or contest, but should he do so the pleasure of achievement will remain with him for a very long time.

The Hand Throw to the Front (Ma-Mae Tewaza)

This is used against an opponent who is moving to his front, or who pushes at you with his hands. He may even do both. The throw is made in the direction in which he is moving. As in all throws made to the opponent's front, an essential preliminary is to remove your own body from his line of advance; otherwise he could not fall even if he wanted to.

In Figure 106A your opponent steps forward with right foot. As he does so, you turn to the left on the ball of your right foot, withdrawing your left hip away from him and swinging your left leg with it (Fig. 106B). Both your knees should be bent. Draw him forward and round with your left arm in the same arc as that taken. by your left hip (Fig. 104). The bending of the left knee gives the downward drive for the throw, the success of which depends on the withdrawal of the left hip. Despite the throw's name, the use of the hands and arms alone will not achieve the desired result.

Draw him forward and around in the same arc as that taken by your left hip. The withdrawal of your hip brings the upper part of his body past the point of balance.

The lowering of the left hip locks your opponent's right foot to the ground, making it impossible for him to recover his balance by advancing it. The withdrawal of the hip draws the upper part of his body forward past the point of balance (Fig. 105). Should your initial attack fail, he will escape you by taking another step forward, but in doing so he lays himself open to a renewed attack, in which you could use the Drawing Ankle Throw.

Fig. 104

Draw him forward and around in the same arc as that taken by your left hip.

Fig. 105

The withdrawl of your hip brings the upper part of his body past the point of balance.

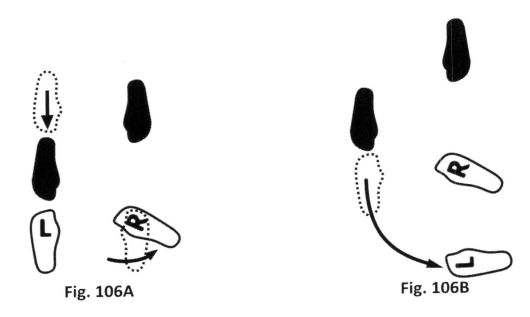

Fig. 106A   **Fig. 106B**

Hand Throw to the Rear (Ma-Ushiro Tewaza)

Fundamentally this throw is the basis of all throws to an opponent's rear. The principle of it is to prevent your opponent from stepping back as you move in to attack. If you fail to stop him in this and persist in attempting the throw, the probability is that you yourself will be thrown from a counter-throw.

The opponent steps back as in Figure 109A. As he does so, you step forward with your left foot, placing it outside his right foot (Fig. 109B). This requires an extra-long step in which the foot should be glided forward over the mat. Do not lunge in. Simultaneously arch your body forward and pin him to the mat on his heels as described in other throws to the rear (Fig. 107). It is most important that you curve your body forward as you step in to break his balance. If you have successfully combined these movements, opponent will be borne over backwards until he lands on his back on the mat.

The action of the hands is important. The left hand drives directly downwards, preferably with the arm straight and the knuckles of the fingers pointing to the mat. That it is not always possible to take the "straight arm" grip, however, may be seen in Figure 107, where the defender is holding so high on the sleeve that the attacker cannot straighten his arm. Figure 29 shows the ideal position.

The right hand retains its hold on opponent's lapel in which position it can drive directly against the shoulder or collar- bone (Fig. 108). You must take care to ensure that this hand does not slide over his shoulder, as can happen if opponent is ,wearing a very loose jacket. If it does, you will lose control and he will escape the throw by stepping back with his left foot.

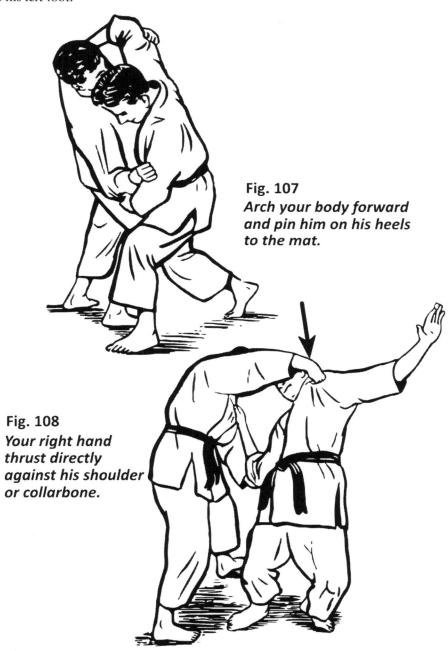

Fig. 107
Arch your body forward and pin him on his heels to the mat.

Fig. 108
Your right hand thrust directly against his shoulder or collarbone.

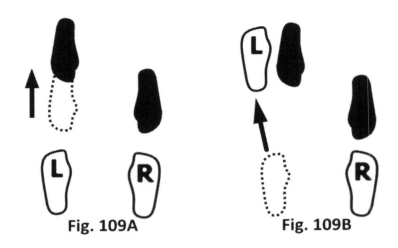

Fig. 109A   Fig. 109B

CHAPTER VI
Hip Throw Group

This group of throws comprises:

1. The Hip Throw

2. The Sweeping Loin Throw

3. The Spring Hip Throw

The Hip Throw is the basic throw of judo and every effort must be made to master it. If this is done, far less difficulty will be met with when attempting not only the other throws of the group, but all judo throws and groundwork. In each of the throws in the Hip Group the final throwing action is made from the hips or loins. It is this movement which sweeps your opponent from the mat and it is the one which presents the most difficulty. The thrust must be made directly backwards, sliding your opponent from the mat. It is fatal to attempt an upward, lifting movement, although you will often see this attempted, sometimes by people whose grade indicates they should know better. The upward thrust requires the thrower to lift his opponent bodily from the mat, thus making the throw more difficult and, in the case of women and boys, almost impossible. The key to success in these throws lies in the maximum withdrawal of your left hip and leg—a full 80° is essential, more is better.

The Hip Throw (Ogoshi)

This is one of the most popular throws with beginners, probably because greater strength can in some measure make up for lack of skill. But this is the worst possible of reasons for favoring any throw, and the novice who finds himself influenced by such considerations must ruthlessly readjust his outlook if his progress is not to be impeded and impaired.

The throw is made against an opponent who is advancing on his right foot or who is thrusting against your right shoulder or chest as he does so. For the throw to be successful, your opponent should n ot be shorter than you are, as this adds considerably to the difficulties of the throw. Against a shorter opponent it is better to use another form of attack.

As your opponent comes forward, assist his advance by pulling him on with an upwards movement of the hands to break his balance. At the same time step forward on to the ball of your right foot, turning to the left (Figs. 110A & 111). You r right foot and his should make a rough letter "L"—see Figure 110A. Arching you r body forward, withdraw your left hip and bring your left leg round to position shown in Figure 110B. Your two feet now should be about the width of your shoulders apart (normally about 18 inches). Your knees must be well bent in order to lower your hips, as the success of the throw depends on your hips being lower than those of your opponent (Fig. 112). Throughout the withdrawal of the left hip, you continue to pivot on your right foot until it has passed through a full 180°. Continue to pull with your left hand and push with your right, following the arc of the hip and curving your body forward as you hold your opponent off balance.

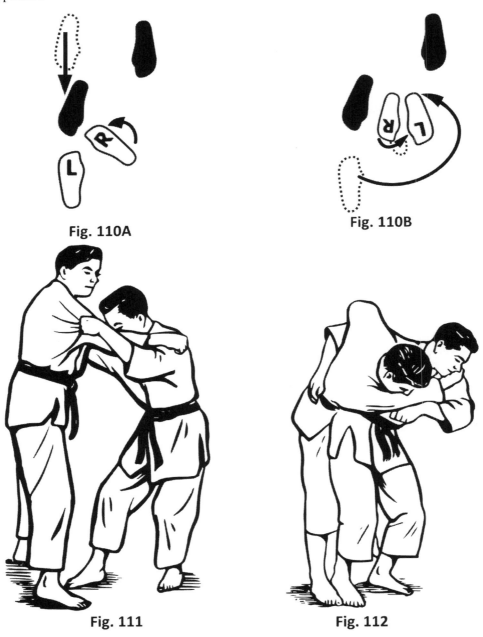

Fig. 110A

Fig. 110B

Fig. 111

Fig. 112

In turning to your left, release your hold with your right hand and pass your arm round his waist, all the time continuing to pull him forward with your left hand. If your timing is correct you will find your turning movement brings your right arm into position almost without any conscious effort on your part. If you force your right arm forward you will destroy the rhythm of your turning movement. Transfer your weight to your left foot and slightly protrude your hips to the right. Retaining the steady pull of your left hand and pressing him firmly against your back with the right, continue to withdraw the left hip until he is lying across you r right hip with only his toes on the mat. Now drive your hips back into him so that his feet are swung clear of the mat (Fig. 113). Continue withdrawing your left hip until your body slides from underneath him and he falls to the mat (Fig. 114). The success of this throw depends on the effective breaking of his balance at the outset when he first steps forward. If you fail in this, the throw cannot be made.

Although it makes it rather more difficult this throw can be made without changing the right-hand position from clasping your opponent's lapel to grasping him round the waist. I prefer this variation because it gives your opponent less warning and enables you to exercise greater control throughout.

Fig. 113

65

Fig. 114

The Sweeping Loin Throw (Harai-Goshi)

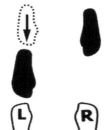

Fig. 115A

Fig. 115B

Fig. 115C

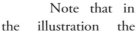

Fig. 115D

The Sweeping Loin is one of the most graceful throws in judo. Basically similar to the Hip Throw, it requires better balance because the throw is made while balanced on one leg only. The opportunity for using it is the same as in the Hip Throw, although in this case it does not matter if your opponent is shorter than you.

As opponent comes forward, pull him in the direction he is moving in and step in with the right foot, turning on it as far as possible to the left (Figs. 115A & B). As you move in, arch your body forward and bend your right knee in order to lower the level of your hips (Fig. 116). Keep pulling him forward and withdraw your left hip, taking your right leg with it until the foot comes to rest with the heel just in front of the toes of your opponent's right foot (Figs. 115C & 117). Transfer your weight to the ball of your left foot with the knee well bent and lean forward, pulling your opponent to you so that he is off balance to his front. Now swing your right leg back—not upwards and sweep his feet clear of the mat. This last movement is actually a backward flick of the right hip, the back of the leg making contact with opponent's right leg at about knee level (Fig. 115D).

Note that in the illustration the thrower has slipped his right arm round his opponent's waist as he did for the Hip Throw.

Fig. 116

67

While this is no doubt the easiest way for the beginner, the more experienced man will retain his hold on the lapel, keeping his right arm close to him, rather as if he were using a boxing right-hook to his opponent's jaw. He uses this arm to drive up and to his left in a circular motion following the arc of the left hip.

Fig. 117
Keep pulling him forward, withdrawing your left hip and taking your right leg with it until the foot comes to rest just in front of the toes of his right foot.

Fig. 118
As you sweep his feet away, continue to turn to your left, driving him forward over your leg.

The Spring Hip Throw (Hane-Goshi)

This is an excellent judo exercise for beginners, though it is too difficult for them to attempt in combat. It is really a contest throw for Black Belts only, but because it is spectacular most novices are early tempted to try it. Although close contact between the two bodies at the moment of throwing is important in all throws in the "Hip" group, in the present instance it is imperative.

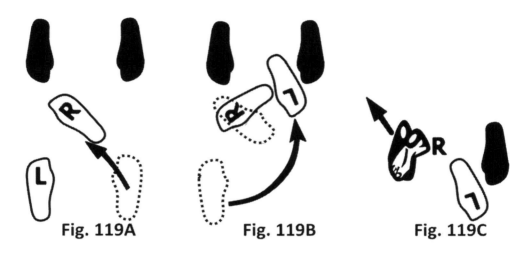

Fig. 119A   **Fig. 119B**   **Fig. 119C**

Opportunity for the throw arises when an opponent thrusts forward at you, preferably moving straight ahead rather than to his right front or left front corners.

Step forward with your right foot, turning on it to the left (Fig. 119A). At the same time use both hands to draw your opponent forward to break his balance to his front, lifting him slightly with the wrists (Fig. 120). Maintain this lift and forward pull throughout the throw.

As you turn on your right foot, withdraw the left hip and take your left leg back, and with knee well bent place it on the mat close up to your opponent's left foot (Fig. 119B). Transfer your balance to your left foot and set the instep of your right foot low against his right shin (Figs. 119C & 121). The pull of your arms should now have brought your opponent into close contact with your body so that every movement you make is transmitted to him.

Keeping your left knee bent and leaning forward, continue turning to the left and simultaneously drive his right leg away by thrusting back—not up—with your right hip (Figs. 122 & 123). Although in the course of this throw you sweep your opponent from the mat, at no time do you actually lift him.

Again, the illustrations show the thrower with his arm right around his opponent's waist. As in the other throws in this group, this method is easier for the beginner, but I prefer to see the throw made with the right hand retaining its grip on the lapel throughout.

Fig. 120

Fig. 121

Fig. 122

Fig. 123

71

The Inner Thigh Throw (Uchi-Mata)

This is not a throw for beginners and is only included here because, like the Stomach Throw, it is the throw most people have heard about and most novices want to try. The trouble arises when the novice does not know the correct procedure and is tempted to improvise. Therein lies the danger in throws such as this. Inexpertly executed they can result in injury; considerable judo practice and experience are necessary to achieve the required standard of proficiency to remove risk of accident.

The Inner Thigh Throw is made usually against an opponent who is on the defensive. His weight should be forward, knees well bent, his arms holding you off stiffly (Fig. 124). The throw should never be used against an opponent whose weight is back or moving back.

The opponent is on the defensive (Fig. 124), or moves forward on his right foot (Fig. 125A). You meet him by stepping in with your right foot, placing it close up to. his (Fig. 125A). As you move in, your body is arched forward, your foot is turned to the left as far as it will comfortably go, and you use your arms and wrists to lift him a little and pull him power- fully towards you in a single movement. Continue to turn on your right foot, with- drawing your left hip until the foot has described a full half-circle into position B, Figure 125. Transfer your weight from right foot to left foot and, in an unbroken movement, sweep your right leg between his legs (Fig 125C), pulling him tight up against you so that you are in close body contact with him (Fig. 126). Sweep back with your right hip in a similar action to the Spring Hip Throw (Fig. 127), your right thigh against the inside of his left thigh.

Your right knee must have been bent from the beginning, and your body turned through a full 180°. In the final movement, on no account must you sweep upwards with your legs as this can be extremely painful to your opponent and spoils the throw because you cannot complete your turn to the left. Another possible cause of injury comes from falling on your opponent. This must be avoided at all costs even though it means your losing the throw.

Fig. 124

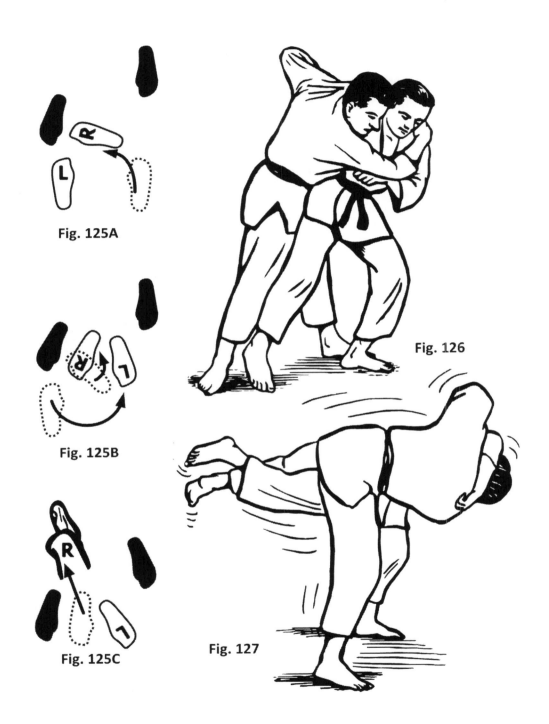

Fig. 125A

Fig. 125B

Fig. 125C

Fig. 126

Fig. 127

74

CHAPTER VII
Leg Throws

Of the three throws included in this group; one, the Body Drop, is officially classified as a Hand Throw. As, however, the distinction is purely academic and the Body Drop is more akin to the Leg Throws, I have included it under the present head.

These throws are effected against an opponent who holds you off with stiff arms, making it difficult for you to obtain the close body contact required for a Hip Throw. They are just as effective as Hip Throws, but are not easy for the beginner to put into effective practice.

The Body Drop (Taiotoshi)

Fig. 128

In Figure 128 your opponent is holding you off with stiff arms and is leaning forward to escape a possible ankle or hip throw. You can either attack when he is in this position or wait for him to step forward with his right foot (Fig. 129A). In either case step in with your right foot, taking as long a pace as your opponent's stiff arms will allow (Fig. 130). You must, however, be careful not to force your way in as, if you do, you may lose your balance backwards. As part of the same movement turn your foot well to the left and pull opponent to his front. Next bring your hip into play, withdrawing it to the left in a circular motion as you turn on the ball of your right foot, allowing your left leg to follow in the same arc. Your left foot should come to rest in the position shown in Figure 129C—that is, in front of opponent's left foot, with toes turned out slightly to the left. Figure 131 shows the relative position of the two contestants at this stage.

Throughout this turn your knees must be appreciably bent and you must keep pulling your opponent to his front with your left hand. Meanwhile your right hand assists the left by pushing in the arc followed by your left hip.

As your left foot comes into position transfer your weight to it and at once slide your right foot across the mat until the back of your leg just above the heel presses firmly against his right shin (Figs. 129D & 132). From this posit ion both your arms drive him to the mat over your outstretched leg as your left hip continues to withdraw.

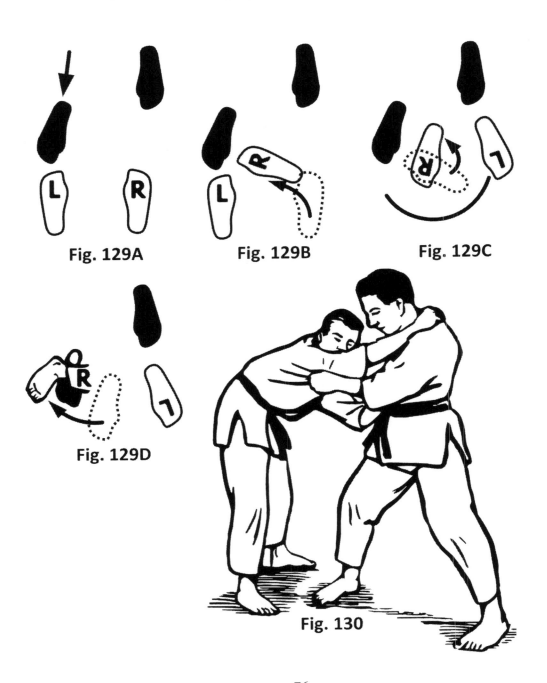

Fig. 129A

Fig. 129B

Fig. 129C

Fig. 129D

Fig. 130

Fig. 131

Fig. 132

77

Body Drop to the Side (Yoko Taiotoshi)

This is a simplified version of the Body Drop; suitable circumstances are essential to its successful performance. Assume your opponent is holding you off with arms stiff and suddenly sidesteps to his right. Follow his movement by stepping to your left with your left foot and turning on it to the left. With a "steering wheel" action of the two hands drive him downwards to his right (Fig. 133).

To retain his balance, he must take another step to his right. As he makes to do so, reach out your right leg and press it back as low as possible against the outside of his right leg (Fig. 134). Continuing the "steering wheel" action of the arms, throw him over your extended leg. If your opponent is heavy, it sometimes helps if you turn to your left as you make the final movement.

Fig. 133

Fig. 134

The Leg Wheel Throw (Ashi-Guruma)

In theory the Leg Wheel Throw is very similar to the Body Drop. It is generally used against an opponent advancing to the front in a defensive posture, but may also be used against one who is standing still with his feet level. Slightly modified, it can also be highly effective to the side.

In Figure 135A your opponent moves in with his right foot, possibly also thrusting forward with his right arm. You counter by stepping in with your right foot, turning on it to the left (Fig. 135B), and pulling. him forward with a lifting action of the arms. Withdraw your left hip and continue to pivot on the ball of y our right foot, allowing your left foot to follow the arc of the hip until it comes to rest with the heel just in front of opponent's left toes (Fig. 135C). As you turn, continue to pull with your left hand and push with the right (Fig. 136) so that both forces are working in the direction taken by the left hip.

In this position he must step forward with his right foot if he is to retain his balance, and to forestall this you press the back of your right leg just above the heel against his right leg just below the knee (Figs. 135 & 137). (In Figure 137 the thrower's body should be turned more to his left to help the turn of his hips.) The throw follows as pressing strongly back from the hip—not the knee—and maintaining the pressure of your hands, you continue to turn to your left.

As mentioned above, this throw can be modified to counter an opponent who is moving to the side or, maybe, who offers strong resistance by bending his knees and pulling powerfully backwards. Figure 138 shows opponent having moved sideways to the right. You follow by stepping to your left and driving him further to your left with your hands. Your right hand imparts an upward movement to the left; your left a downward movement to the left. His natural reaction is to step to his right again in order to recover, and you prevent this by placing the back of your right leg, just above the heel, in front of his right leg (Fig. 139). Press back with your right leg and drive forward with you r arms and he will be thrown.

Should he try to escape the throw by leaning back, slip your right foot round his leg till it presses against the back of his knee (Fig. 140). Drive him backwards and downwards with your arms.

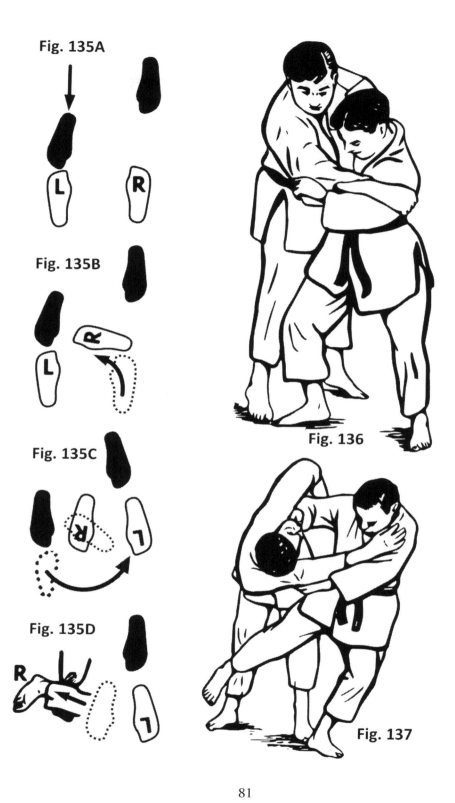

Fig. 135A

Fig. 135B

Fig. 135C

Fig. 135D

Fig. 136

Fig. 137

Fig. 138

Fig. 139

Fig. 140

The Knee Wheel Throw (Hiza-Guruma)

Although this throw has points of similarity to the Drawing Ankle Throw, the two must not be confused, and any attempt to combine them will certainly end in failure. In the one you attack the ankle, in the other the knee—or immediately below it. If your attacking foot makes contact, say, halfway down your opponent's shin, you will have insufficient leverage to make the throw.

The Knee Wheel is used against an opponent on the defensive. Persuade him to take a forward step; if he does so with his right foot, throw him with a right-handed throw. In Figure 141A opponent has advanced his right foot. Pull him forward with an upward lift of the arms, take a tiny step forward with your right foot, turning on it to the left (Fig. 141B). (Some instructors recommend that this short step should be taken to the right rather than the front (Fig. 142). As you move your right foot, turn to your left by withdrawing your left hip and push with your right hand in the same arc. (See arrows in Figure 142.) This should break his balance to his front and his defence must be a further step with his right foot.

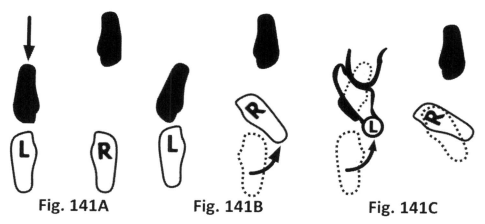

Fig. 141A   **Fig. 141B**   **Fig. 141C**

To prevent this, bring your left foot up and press the sole against your opponent's right leg just below the knee (Figs.141c & 143). In this position your left leg should be straight and your right leg slightly bent at the knee to lower the hips and maintain maximum balance. In Figure 143 the Thrower's right knee could be a little more bent to advantage and his body more upright. Continue to turn to the left and wheel your opponent over your extended foot.

It is important in this throw to watch the positioning of the left foot on opponent's leg. If it is too high, opponent will be able to brace his knee against your thrust; if too low, you will not have sufficient leverage to bring him to the mat.

Fig. 142

Fig. 143

84

CHAPTER VIII
The Shoulder Throw Group

This group comprises some of judo's most graceful and spectacular throws. With the exception of the Shoulder Drop, they are mostly used by the shorter of two contestants.

Close body contact is essential to their successful execution, and before this can be achieved your opponent's balance must be effectively broken. If this is neglected a counter-throw will be the probable result. The other essentials to success are that the thrower's knees be well bent in order to bring his hips well below the level of those of the opponent, and that the thrower's body be curved forward in order to develop maximum power. This arching of the body also has the effect of making him less vulnerable to counter attack to his rear as he turns.

The Shoulder Throw Using the Arm (Seoinage)

This is the best known and easiest to perform of the shoulder throws and is an excellent counter against blows aimed at head or face in an unexpected rough house outside judo circles. Within judo, it is frequently used against a thrusting opponent who advances, say, with his right foot and pushes at you with his right hand.

Fig. 144

As opponent moves in, step forward with your right foot, turning the foot as far to the left as you can comfortably manage (Fig. 144). Draw him on in the direction he is moving with an upward lift of both hands. Note that the toes of your right foot are close against the toes of his right foot. Your body should be bowed slightly forward to produce maximum power. On no account must you lean back to make contact with your opponent as this will invite a counter-throw to your rear.

As your right foot comes to the ground, bend your knee and withdraw your left hip, swinging your left foot with it so that it almost brushes the right foot and comes to rest level with the right foot twelve to eighteen inches from it. Halfway through this turn release your right-hand hold of your opponent's jacket, but continue to pull with your left. The correct pull is now more important than ever, since you are holding with only one hand. Continuing the turn, bring your right arm under his right arm in a sort of scooping action (Fig.145) and wind it round his arm as shown in Figure 146. Figure 147 shows the foot movement.

Transfer your balance to your left leg and thrust your hips back into him. The thrust must be back, not upward. By leaning slightly forward you will throw him off balance and by thrusting back you will sweep him off the ground. Continue your turn to the left to complete the throw.

Fig. 145

Fig. 146

Fig. 147

The Shoulder Throw Using the Jacket (Moroteseoi Nage)

Fig. 148

I recommend this shoulder throw to all beginners although it is rather more difficult to execute than the preceding one.

The leg and foot movements are identical with those already described and so are the arm movements for the first half of the throw. The difference arises in that you do not leave go of his lapel with your right hand. Instead you bend your wrist forward and drive upward and round in the direction of the arrows shown in Figure 148, as though you were trying to punch yourself on the jaw with your right fist. When your turn to the left is so far completed that your back is in close contact with your opponent's chest, press your right elbow forcefully up into his right armpit (Fig. 149). The upward thrust of your elbow prevents your opponent from escaping by stepping or sliding round you, and is the chief advantage of this throw. Figure 149 is drawn from an action photograph of the brilliant international John Chaplin; the position would have been better if the left foot had been a shade further back, and the right a little further forward. Note the well-bent knees and how the body is curved forward to give maximum efficiency but is not crouched.

The throw is completed in a similar manner to the Shoulder Throw Using the Arm. Pay particular care to keep your body bowed forward. If you lean back to make contact as the judoka is doing in Figure 150, you are certain to be countered. You can get into a similar ineffective position by endeavouring to make body contact too early in the throw—that is, before your opponent's balance has been broken. This is a most common error.

Fig. 149

Fig. 150

The Shoulder Drop Throw (Seio-Otoshi)

This is not a true shoulder throw and I would only recommend it to the tall beginner whose height makes it difficult for him to find partners with whom to practise the true shoulder throws. Strictly, I would place it among the Leg Throws, since it looks like a modification of the Body Drop, but because of its name and classification I have included it in the present group. It is used against an advancing opponent or one who is stationary but is pushing forward aggressively with his arms.

Your opponent advances his right foot (Fig. 151A) and you counter by moving to position Figure 151B, disturbing his balance with a forward pull as you do so. Withdraw your left hip, turning on the ball of the right foot. Pull with your left hand and push with your right in the same arc as taken by your left hip. Continue to turn until your feet are in the position shown in Figure 151C. Halfway through the turn, let go with your right hand and pass it under his arm (Fig. 152).

Because you are the taller man (you would not otherwise be attempting this throw) you cannot lower your hips sufficiently to get under your opponent as shown in Figure 146. Instead, pull his arm for- ward with your left hand and wind your right arm round his upper arm (Fig. 153).

In this position, because you cannot get directly underneath his body, it would be easy for him to slide or step round you as you continue to turn to the left. To prevent this, as soon as your left foot reaches position 151C, transfer your weight to it and extend your right leg back to press against the outside of his right foot (Figs. 151D & 154). Your continued turning to the left and the persistent pull of your arms will affect the final throw.

Some people prefer to grasp opponent's right sleeve with both hands (Fig. 155) instead of the method described above, but it is not a method I personally favour although it is perhaps the better-known version of the throw.

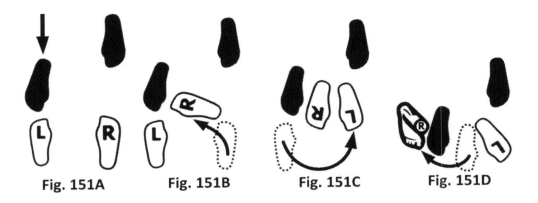

Fig. 151A   Fig. 151B   Fig. 151C   Fig. 151D

Fig. 152

Fig. 153   Fig. 154

Fig. 155

CHAPTER IX
Sacrifice Throws

It is a popular belief in some quarters that Sacrifice Throws are so called because the thrower sacrifices his own balance in order to make the throw. This is quite wrong; no experienced judoka would ever willingly sacrifice his balance. He will, however, sacrifice his upright posture when the occasion warrants, and it is from this that these throws get their name. Sacrifice throws are divided into two sections—those in which the thrower is left lying on his side at the completion of the throw, and those in which he finishes lying on his back. There are many throws in each category, all of them spectacular and effective and all of them potentially dangerous. Because of their potential danger I propose to include only one of these throws in this book—the Stomach Throw—which is classified under the second of the two subdivisions.

The Stomach Throw (Tomoenage)

Free practice of this throw is banned by many clubs because it requires considerable unrestricted space for performance in safety. The student should therefore consult his club's rules before attempting to practise it. The strict interpretation of its Japanese name is "throwing in a circle," a very apt description of the movements it comprises. The opportunity for its use is most likely to occur Fig. 160 when your opponent leans forward and pushes you off in an effort to avoid a Leg, Ankle or Hip throw (Fig. 156). As he pushes forward, step in as close as possible to him, trying to place your left foot as nearly as you can midway between his feet (Fig. 157).

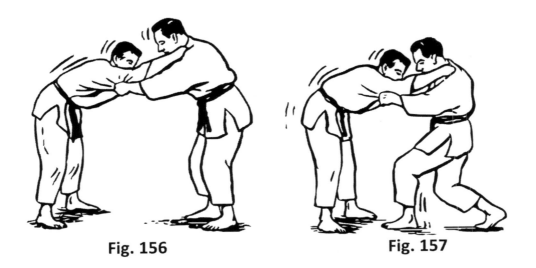

Fig. 156   **Fig. 157**

Accompany this movement by pulling him forward, lifting him if he is shorter than you (Fig. 158), and pulling down if he is taller (Fig. 159).

Fig. 158

Fig. 159

Whether lifting or pulling the wrists provide the motive power. Maintaining this pull on his jacket, squat back on your left heel as if you were about to perform a backward breakfall (Fig. 160), bowing your opponent over you. Now place your right foot against his stomach so that the toes are just below his belt (Fig. 161). Use this leg, still bent at the knee, to swing him over you in a circle as you roll backwards (Fig. 162). Do not straighten the leg or attempt to kick him clear, as this will break the circle and ruin the throw. It might also injure your opponent, or make him fall heavily on top of you. Continue to roll backwards (Fig. 163) until he is thrown just clear of you, falling on his back (Fig. 164).

Fig. 160

Fig. 161

Fig. 162

Throughout the throw your arms must maintain a steady pull on his jacket, though opinion is divided as to whether or not the hands should release their grip as opponent strikes the mat. I recommend they should hold on throughout (Fig. 164). By so doing the thrower retains full control, prohibits the possibility of last-minute evasive action and, if the throw is not sufficiently clean to score a point, he is in an advantageous position from which to the position when the renew his attack. Figure 165 shows the position when the victim has been thrown clear and attacker's grasp relaxed.

Fig. 163

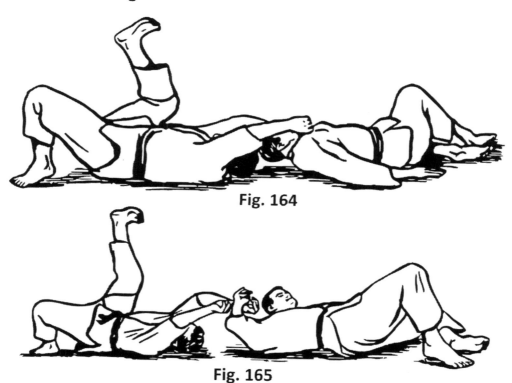

Fig. 164

Fig. 165

CHAPTER X
Holding Down

In contest judo, a contestant is awarded a point if he can hold his opponent down on his back for a period of thirty seconds, while maintaining control of at least one of the opponent's limbs. It is not necessary that the opponent's shoulders be pinned to the ground—as is required in some forms of wrestling—nor even that he should be held flat on his back. It is sufficient solely to hold him down and retain control of an arm or leg.

In the performance of hold-downs certain points should be carefully observed:

1. As in every other judo movement, the whole body must always be comfortably relaxed.

2. The main weight of the attacker's body should be on the mat—not on his opponent. Figure 166 shows attacker's weight centred in his thigh and right hip. In this position his balance is secure and not likely to be disturbed by the victim's struggles. Figure 167 shows the wrong position. Here, every movement the victim makes is transmitted to the attacker, making it comparatively easy for the victim to unbalance the attacker and throw him off by rolling over (Fig. 168).

Fig. 166

3. Once the hold has been applied, attacker must maintain the same relative position between himself and his opponent. He must therefore follow every move the victim makes, thus ensuring that his present secure balance is not jeopardized.

96

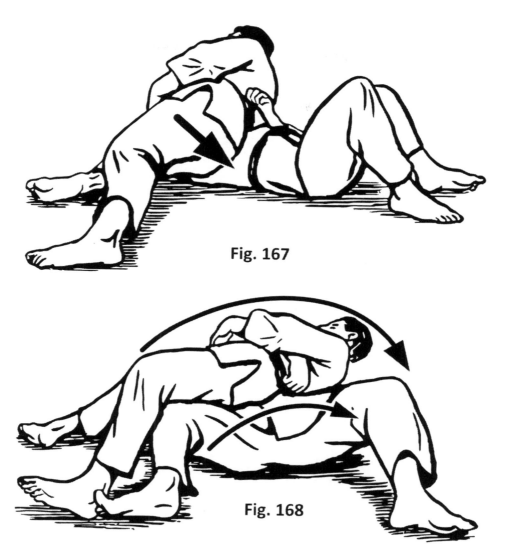

Fig. 167

Fig. 168

4.   To achieve "3" above, it is essential that the attacker's posture on the mat should be both poised and flexible. A camera on a tripod gives a fair analogy of this (Fig. 169). Maximum stability of the camera is achieved when the legs of the tripod are spread at just the right angle. If the angle is too great the legs lose some of their rigidity and may collapse under the camera's weight; if the angle is too small there is a serious loss in stability of balance and danger of the camera toppling to the ground.

In judo hold-downs, the same rules apply. The legs of the tripod are formed by the attacker's two legs and his hips (Fig. 170). If the attacker spreads his legs as wide as he can with comfort and relaxation he will be in the position of maximum efficiency, able to counter and control every move made by his opponent. Note that "comfort" is the yardstick in this as in all judo movement. If an action or posture is not comfortable, it is because some muscle or other is under strain or tension, a condition which makes complete relaxation impossible.

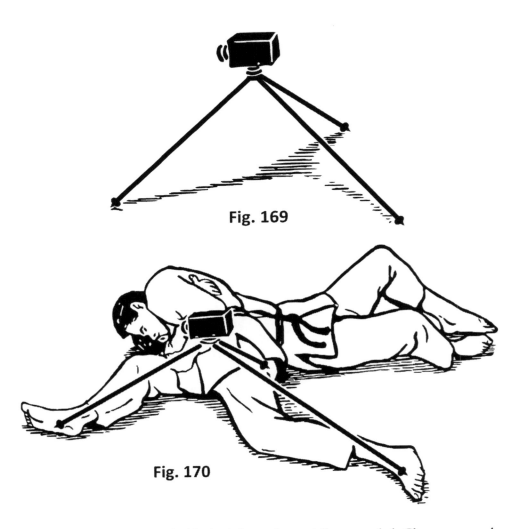

Fig. 169

Fig. 170

5.   Never persist with a hold which has only partially succeeded. Change to another one or break away and get up as soon as you realize you have not complete control of your opponent's movements. Failure to do this may quickly result in the tables being turned and yourself becoming the victim.

6.   Always be on the watch for a chance to apply an arm-lock or stranglehold when you are holding down because in the course of his struggles your opponent may well give you just the opening you require.

The Scarf Hold (Kesagatame)

This is probably the most popular hold in judo. It is one of the most effective and is usually the first to be learned.

Your opponent is lying on his back as the result of your throw which was not sufficiently clean to score you a point. You are still holding on to his right sleeve (Fig. 171). Pull the sleeve towards you with your left hand and place your right foot close to his body to prevent him rolling towards you (Fig. 172) with the possible consequence of freeing his right arm. Slide your left leg back and drop to the mat with legs widely spread to give you a firm base. As you do so, pull his arm round your left side, pinning it beneath your arm against your thigh and abdomen (Fig. 173).

Figure 174 shows an alternative position with the attacker bent forward so that his head is close up to the opponent's face.

Fig. 171

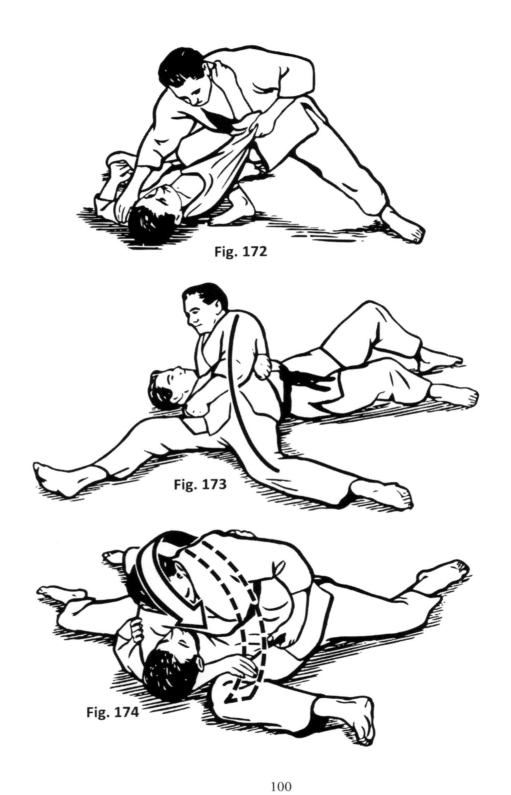

Fig. 172

Fig. 173

Fig. 174

There are four accepted positions for the right arm, any of which you are at liberty to use, though I personally prefer the first.

1.   Pass your arm round his neck and grip your own trousers just above your right knee (Fig. 175). This hold gives excellent security against opponent's struggles and has the advantage of being easily changed to one of the alternative positions should the situation warrant it.

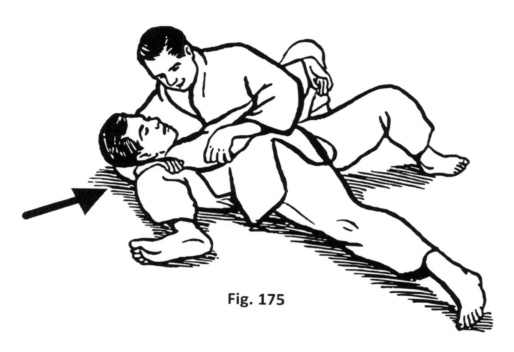

Fig. 175

2. Pass your arm round his neck as before and grip his jacket just behind his right shoulder (Fig. 176). This hold is also excellent because your grip of his jacket gives you greater control of his body as he twists and turns in an effort to escape.

Fig. 176

3. Place your right hand on the mat, palm down, either close up against opponent's head (Fig. 177), or in a straight line out from your shoulder (Fig. 178). The advantage of these two variations is that escape by rolling to the left, or by victim rolling you over the top of him, is almost impossible.

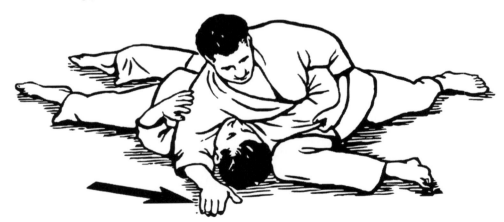

Fig. 177

Fig. 178

4.   Grip opponent's jacket under the left armpit (Fig. 179). This hold is much
favored by the Americans, but is not often seen outside the United States. It is
easy to change from it to the previous alternative version in case of necessity.

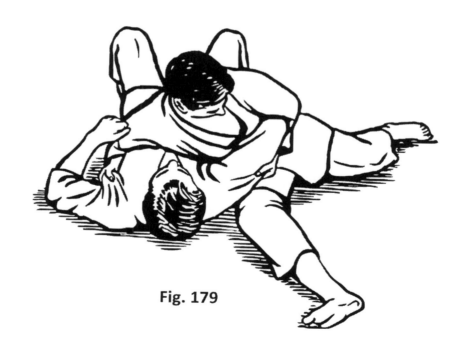

Fig. 179

Whichever hold with the right hand you elect to use, never hesitate to change it for one of the others should it be expedient to do so. Apply only sufficient weight and strength to overcome your opponent's struggles or to master a counter attack. If he moves about the mat in his efforts to get free, move with him, staying in the same relative position in which you started—i.e. with your right knee close to his right ear.

Side Four-Quarter Hold Down (Yokoshihogatame)

This hold, as its name implies, is made from your opponent's side. Fig. 180 gives the general picture. Opponent is lying on his back and you are face down to him, your two bodies roughly making a letter "T". Your left arm is under his neck and gripping his jacket at the left shoulder (Fig. 181), while your right arm passes between his legs, the hand grasping his belt at his back (Figs. 181 & 182). It is important that your right arm should pass between his legs high up in the crutch; otherwise he will be able to use the full force of his thigh muscles against your arm, making it impossible for you to hold on (Fig. 184).

Your own legs should be fully extended and spread apart so as to make the "tripod" as secure as possible. Your hips should be down on the mat and, if you have to press forward to prevent opponent from raising his left side, do so from the toes—not the knees (Fig. 183). Whatever his movements, you must keep the original relative position of your two bodies (Fig.180).

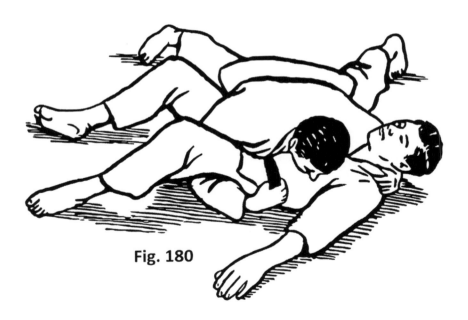

Fig. 180

104

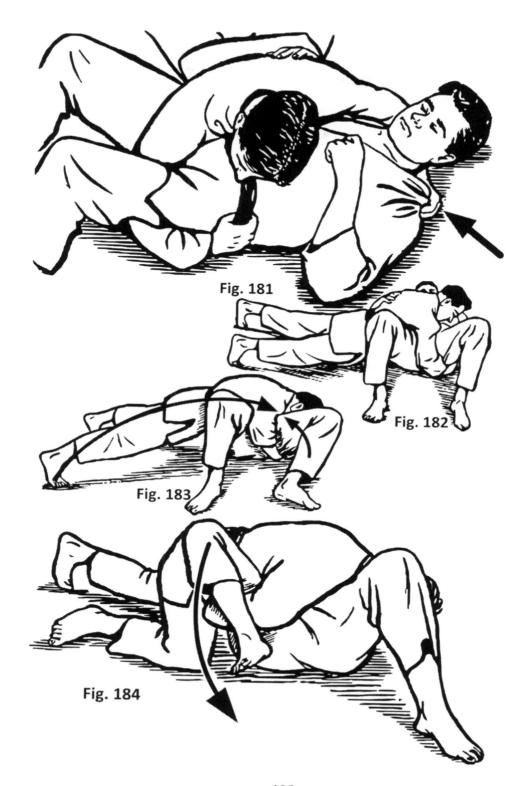

Fig. 181

Fig. 182

Fig. 183

Fig. 184

Side Four-Quarter (Alternative Version)

This alternative technique in the Side Four-Quarter is commonly used, though I consider it less strong and therefore less effective. The basic position is identical with that shown in Fig. 180 with the exception that the attacker draws his knees up to his opponent's side instead of extending them. As before, the legs are well spread and control comes from the toes (Fig. 185).

A valid objection to this hold is that it does not conform to the basic rule which says that the hips must retain contact with the ground. However, though the hips are clear of the ground, it is possible to keep them sufficiently low to make the hold not ineffective.

Fig. 185

Side Four-Quarter (Second Alternative Version)

This is similar to the first variation except that you draw up only one leg—whichever you choose—leaving the other extended (Fig. 186). If the left leg is extended it gives you greater control of your opponent's shoulders; if the right leg, greater control of his hips (Fig. 187).

Speaking from experience, I am of the opinion that neither of the alternative versions is a match for the original.

106

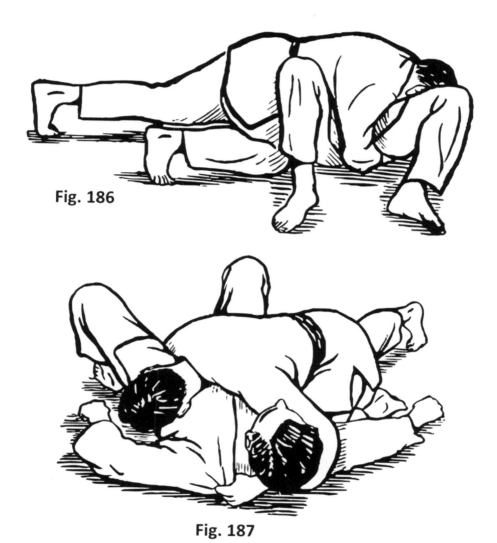

Fig. 186

Fig. 187

The Upper Four-Quarter Hold Down (Kamishihogatame)

This is a very powerful hold and an excellent reason why you should never let an opponent get behind you. Once behind you, if he applies the Upper Four-Quarter, you will not easily escape.

In Fig. 188 your opponent is lying on his back. You have approached from behind his head and are lying extended with your chest on his, your elbows pressing hard into his armpits, your hands holding his belt on either side. Your head is turned to one side and pressing down on him; your hips are on the ground. Your legs should be widespread equally to either side so that his body and your legs together form a letter "Y". The reason for this is that should he succeed in working his body into line with one of your legs (Fig. 189), you will not be able to stop him rolling over to that side (Fig. 190), and breaking your hold.

Glancing back at Fig. 188, it is apparent that the attacker's h old would be much stronger if he were lying actually on his victim's head. But this can be very uncomfortable for the man underneath and is a technique that is better reserved for serious contest.

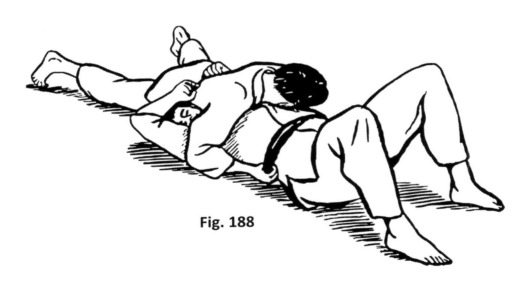

Fig. 188

108

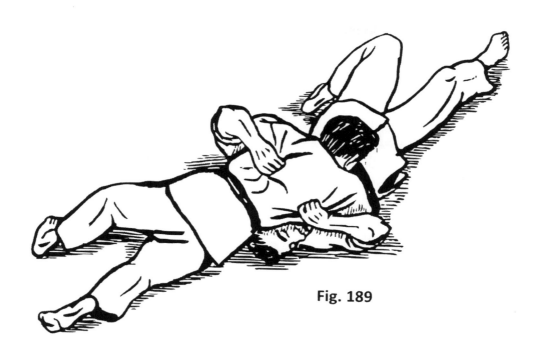

Fig. 189

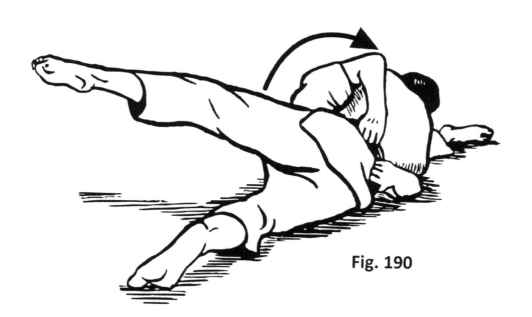

Fig. 190

109

Alternative Positions of the Hands

1. Instead of placing your elbows into his armpits, pass your forearms under his upper-arms and grasp his belt (Fig. 191). Some schools claim that this method gives better control of his arms, but I am not persuaded of it.

2. Adopt either of the described arm positions with your right arm. Your left arm, however, leads straight back under his left shoulder and the hand grasps the back of his collar (Fig. 192). Note that in this alternative hold the attacker's legs do not make a letter "Y" with his opponent's body. In this instance the attacker's body is canted off at an angle to his opponent's body, the angle occurring on the opposite side to the arm which leads back to grasp the opponent's collar (Fig. 192). If the positions of the hands were reversed so that the attacker's right hand was grasping the collar, the legs would then be canted to the left.

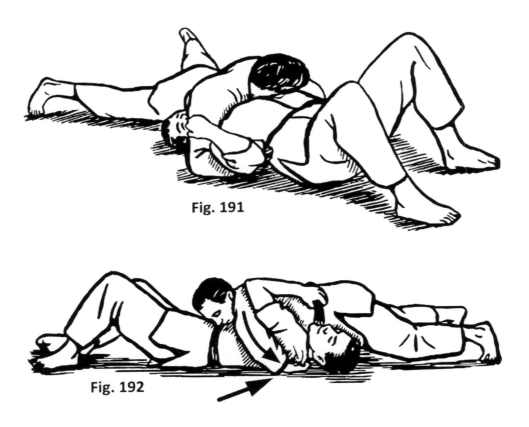

Fig. 191

Fig. 192

110

Alternative Positions of the Legs

These alternatives are somewhat similar to those used in the Side Four-Quarter hold. Both legs may be drawn up (Fig. 193) or one leg drawn up (Fig. 194). If you lie to the left of your opponent's head (his left) you should use a left-hand grip on the back of your opponent's collar and draw up your left leg keeping the inside of the leg flat on the mat. You cannot draw up your right because his head is in the way. Personally, I feel more comfortable with my left leg drawn up than with both legs outstretched. If you lie on the other side of your opponent's head the movements are reversed.

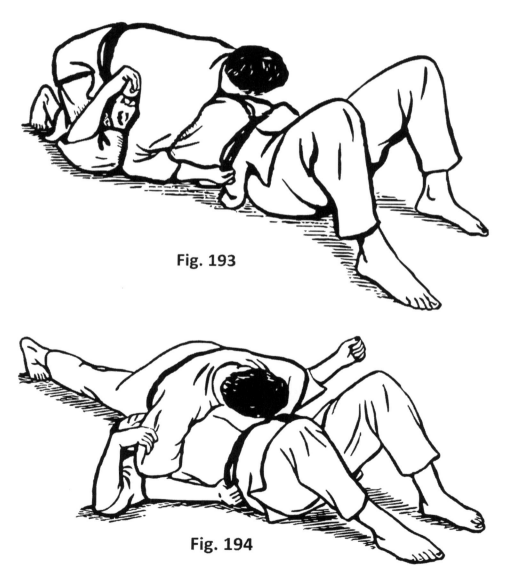

Fig. 193

Fig. 194

The Broken Upper Four-Quarter Hold (Kuzure-Kamishihogatame)

One of the most powerful holds in judo. In execution it follows closely the Upper Four-Quarter Hold as described above under the second of the alternative hand positions. Figure 195 shows the position of the two contestants; the attacker's left arm is leading back under the opponent's left arm and gripping his collar as far round as it can reach (Fig. 197). The right arm takes up the hold shown in Figure 195. Both arms must press well up into the opponent's armpits, so robbing him of much of his effective strength.

Both legs must be fully extended and, as in the Upper Four-Quarter Hold-Down (Second Alternative Position of the Hands), the body must be set up at an angle to your opponent's body. But in this instance the angle is much greater. In Figure 196, the attacker's body lies at an angle of a full 45° to his opponent and on the same side as the arm which is attacking his opponent's collar. The attacker's legs are well spread out to his rear, with toes digging into the mat for greater control. His hips, also, are down on the mat. In Figure 197, the attacker's hips are shown clear of the mat; this is wrong but was purposely drawn so in order not to mask the position of the hand on the collar.

Fig. 195

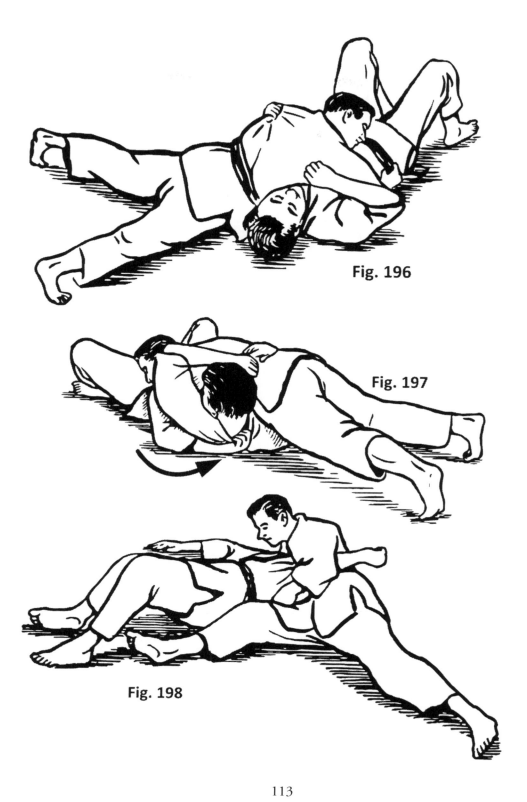

Fig. 196

Fig. 197

Fig. 198

The Reverse Scarf Hold (Gyaku-Kesagatame)

This is not an easy hold to learn but once mastered it is one of the strongest and is my own favorite. It can be applied direct but usually it is used as a follow-up to an unsuccessful Upper Four-Quarter or Broken Upper Four-Quarter, and this is how I shall describe it.

Opponent is lying on his back and you take up the Broken Four-Quarter position (Fig. 196), your right hand grasping his belt, your left doubled back under his arm and firmly grasping his collar well to the back of his neck. Now turn on to your right side by pivoting on your hip to swing your extended right leg to the right until it lies close alongside his body (Fig. 198). His left arm is now securely immobilized under your upper left arm. A wide angle separates your left and right legs.

In this position your victim is so securely held that his only chance of escape is by a backward roll. This you prevent by leaning forward to pin him down by pressing the side of your head firmly on to his abdomen (Fig. 199). Personally, I only use my head in this manner when my opponent forces me to do so, preferring to hold him with my body fairly upright and back well hollowed (Fig. 200). This is sometimes called the Armchair Hold and if you decide to adopt it you must keep alert so that he does not surprise you with a sudden backward roll. If you allow your attention to wander you may get a very painful smack in the face from his knees.

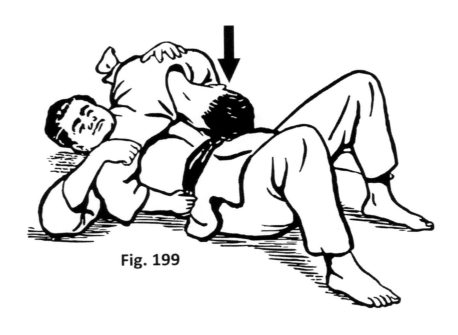

Fig. 199

114

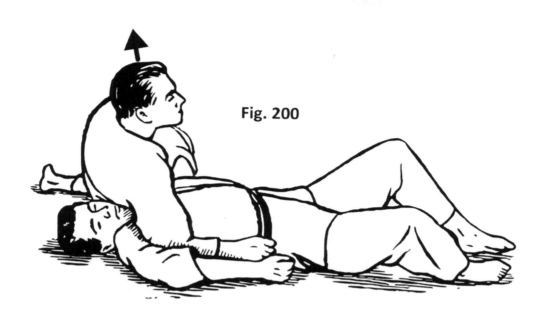

Fig. 200

CHAPTER XI
Strangle Locks and Choke Locks

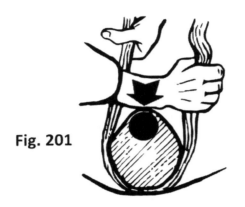

Fig. 201

Fig. 202

Fig. 203

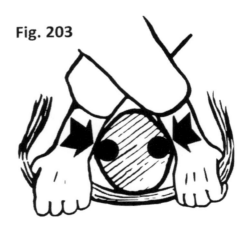

Strangle and choke locks are often lumped together and loosely described as neck locks. Actually, they fall into two distinct classes and the difference between them should be clearly understood. Chokes are applied against the windpipe, the object being to enforce submission by preventing your opponent from breathing (Fig. 201). They are unpleasant to experience but are not as effective as might at first seem because the victim can minimize their effect by using his own hands to relieve the pressure (Fig. 202).

Strangles are applied to the carotid arteries which run down each side of the neck slightly behind the ears (Fig. 203). These arteries are protected by muscles which vary in strength with the individual. The first requirement of the lock is to displace the muscles from their place of protection; when this is done only slight pressure is needed to apply the lock which, if correctly executed, is painless and therefore dangerous. The inexperienced victim may lose consciousness suddenly and unexpectedly often surprising both himself and his attacker.

Submission should therefore be made in plenty of time, and since the victim feels no more pain than a mild discomfort, the decision to break off the attack must often be made by the attacker or the instructor in charge. As the lock takes effect the victim may breathe stertorously and often his body jerks convulsively like an epileptic. Sometimes his face becomes highly flushed but this is by no means an infallible sign. Although to the spectator these symptoms can be rather startling, the victim is conscious of none of them.

Both strangles and chokes can only be effectively applied if you have first gained complete control of your opponent. It is useless to attempt to choke him in the manner of the attacker in Figure 204, for instance, because all the opponent has to do to escape is to turn in the direction in which his jacket is being pulled. In other words, the attacker has not first gained control of the victim's movements before attempting to apply the lock. There are many ways in which this may be done. In Figure 205, the attacker is retaining control by making his two hands work in opposition; in this position the victim is prevented from escaping to the right by the attacker's left arm pulling him in the opposite direction.

Fig. 204   **Fig. 205**

Both strangles and chokes are normally applied by steady pressure of the forearm, the little finger edge, or the thumb edge, of the forearm only being used (Figs. 206 & 207). In the course of the descriptions which follow I shall refer to these edges as the "cutting-edges".

Submission must always be clearly indicated and made in plenty of time. There is no point in holding out to the last moment if you have no chance of breaking free. The

117

customary signal of submission is to tap twice in quick succession on your opponent's body (Fig. 208) or to beat the mat unmistakably with your hand or foot (Fig. 209). Sometimes it is quicker and easier to shout, and this is equally acceptable. All that matters is that your meaning shall be abundantly clear.

When you are the attacker you must release the lock the instant that your opponent submits. It is far better that you should let go too soon in the mistaken belief that he has submitted than hold on too long in the mistaken belief that he is still resisting.

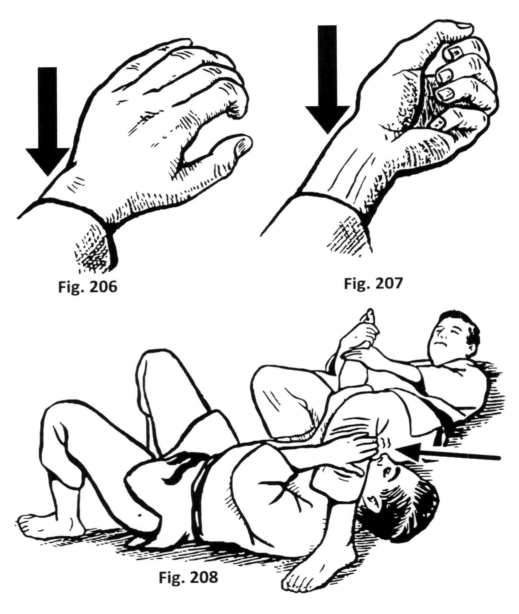

Fig. 206

Fig. 207

Fig. 208

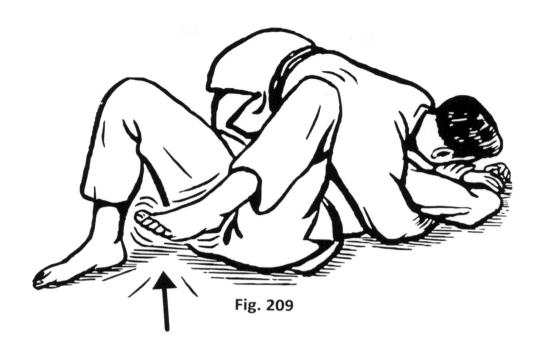

Fig. 209

STRANGLE LOCKS

Complete relaxation is the key to success in all strangles. Unless your arms are fully relaxed they cannot be made to "fit" the shape of your opponent's neck. Your tension will cause your opponent pain though it will place him in no danger of strangulation.

In crossing the arms to take hold of either side of your opponent's collar, it does not matter whether you do so left over right, or right over left. There is an exception to this rule, however, to which your attention is drawn in the Half Cross.

Grip deep down on your opponent's collar with both hands—as close as possible where his back collar stud would normally be. This is much easier said than done, but unless you go deep, particularly in the Normal Cross, the strangle will fail.

The Normal Cross Strangle (Namijugi)

Fig. 210

As this is a lock on the carotid arteries it should cause no unpleasant constriction of the throat. If it produces any such discomfort, it is being wrongly applied.

Sit astride your opponent, with your knees pressing well up into his armpits in order to reduce the effectiveness of his arms. Place your right hand, palm uppermost, as deep into his collar as possible at the right side of his neck. Grip the collar with fingers inside, thumb outside. (In Figure 211, the hand is shown outside the collar for purposes of illustration only.) Your left arm crosses the right and takes a similar grip of the collar on the other side of his neck. Both hands must grasp as deep as possible, the thumb edges of your forearms pressing but not forcing against his neck just below and behind the ears (Fig. 210).

Now press firmly but not vigorously against his neck, and very slowly slide your hands back towards you. This last action should have the effect of moving the protecting muscles forward to expose the arteries to attack. Maintain the pressure and lean forward between your elbows (Fig. 212), if necessary, until your head touches the ground (Fig. 213). Your forearms close like scissors without any conscious assistance from you as your weight comes forward. This should bring about immediate surrender.

Fig. 211

Fig. 212

121

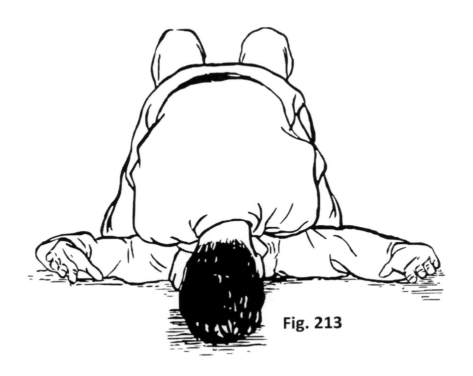

Fig. 213

The Adverse or Reverse Cross (Gyakujujitime)

This lock is very like the Normal Cross but is somewhat easier as the collar holds of the hands comes more easily to most beginners. To offset this, the effect is not so immediate and therefore gives your opponent a few extra moments in which to contrive his escape. In practicing this lock, care should be taken to ensure that it does not change in character from a strangle to a choke.

Take as deep a hold as possible with your right hand, palm down, and a similar hold with your left. Figure 214 shows the left hand outside the jacket for purposes of illustration. As the palms of the hands are downward, it is the little finger cutting-edges which attack opponent's arteries (Fig. 215). The lock is completed exactly as the Normal Cross.

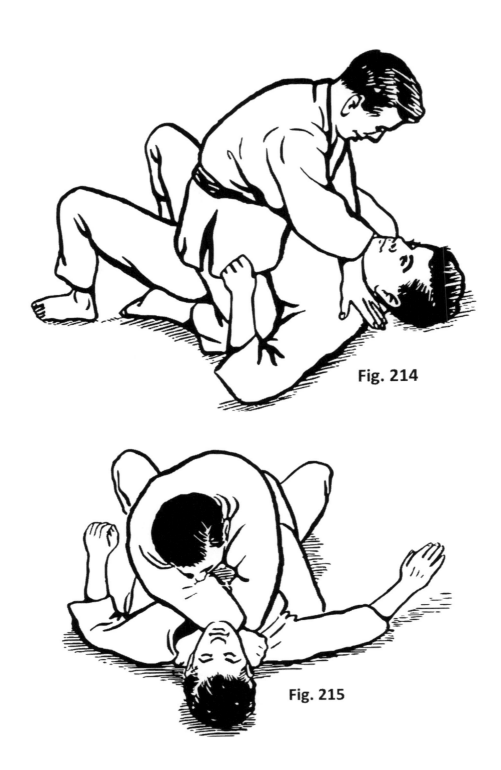

Fig. 214

Fig. 215

The Half Cross (Katajujijime)

As has already been stressed, the main difficulty in all the strangles lies in securing a deep enough hold on your opponent's collar while he is vigorously trying to prevent it. The Half Cross offers a part-solution to this problem, though it also loses in effectiveness in the course of it.

The right hand, palm upwards, grasps the opponent's collar, thumb cutting-edge against the neck (Fig. 216). The left hand passes behind the right hand and takes the "Reverse Cross" grip—i.e. with palm down and little finger cutting-edge against the neck as in the Reverse Strangle. It does not need to go as deep as its partner. In practice, either hand may adopt the reverse hold, but whichever does so must cross behind the hand taking the normal grip.

The final motions are identical with those of the Normal Cross (Fig. 217). Figure 217 is also interesting because it shows the direction of the forces at work not only in this strangle, but in all strangles. For purposes of illustration, Figures 216 and 217 show the hands outside the collar; the actual hold, of course, is made inside the collar.

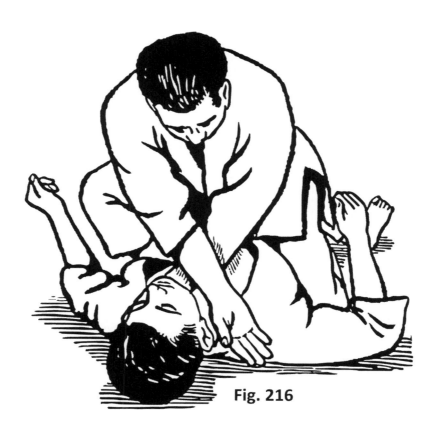

Fig. 216

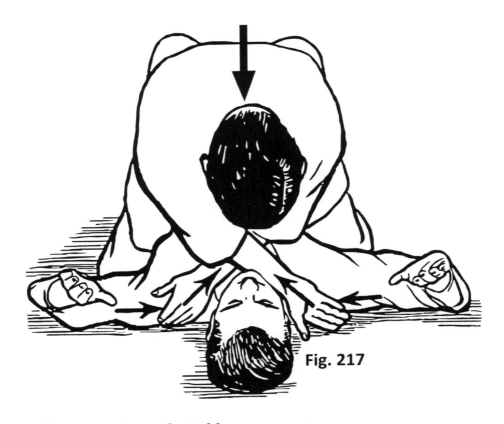

Fig. 217

Final Notes on Strangle Holds

1.   If your strangle does not force submission in about fifteen seconds, you should release it and start again. The only means you have of knowing whether the "sliding forward" action of the forearms has taken effect is by the results produced. If submission has not been made by the end of fifteen seconds you can assume you have failed.

2.   Occasionally you may meet the opponent who has such powerful muscles protecting his carotid arteries that it is virtually impossible to strangle him. When this occurs, it is useless to persist; you will have to resort to some other form of attack.

CHOKE LOCKS

It is sufficient for the beginner to know the three most common choke locks. In the first of these the attack is made from the front and in the other two from behind. The attack from the front is usually effective only against an inexperienced opponent because it is easy to hold off but, given the element of surprise, it can succeed against greater experience and on this account is often worth trying.

The other two locks are important because if you want to use a neck lock on an opponent whose back is towards you, you must use a choke. Strangle Locks from this position must be left to expert judoka because it is extremely difficult to attack the carotid arteries from behind your opponent.

The Cross or Bar Choke (Gatame)

Superficially, this choke has much in common with the "cross" strangles. Indeed, these strangles inexpertly performed often unintentionally develop into Cross Chokes, and with a consequent loss of effectiveness.

You are sitting astride your opponent who is lying supine on the mat. The best attack from this position would be the Adverse Cross Strangle, but because of strong resistance you resort to the Cross Choke. Your right hand, palm down, grips the right side of his collar deep down, the forearm passing under his chin (Fig. 218). Your left hand takes firm grasp of his left lapel (Fig. 219). Take a steady pull on his lapel and bring the little finger cutting-edge of your right forearm into contact with the front of his throat (Fig. 220). Effect the choke by bearing down gently with your right arm; the sole duty of the left hand is to stop your opponent's jacket slipping round under the pull of your right hand.

Fig. 218

127

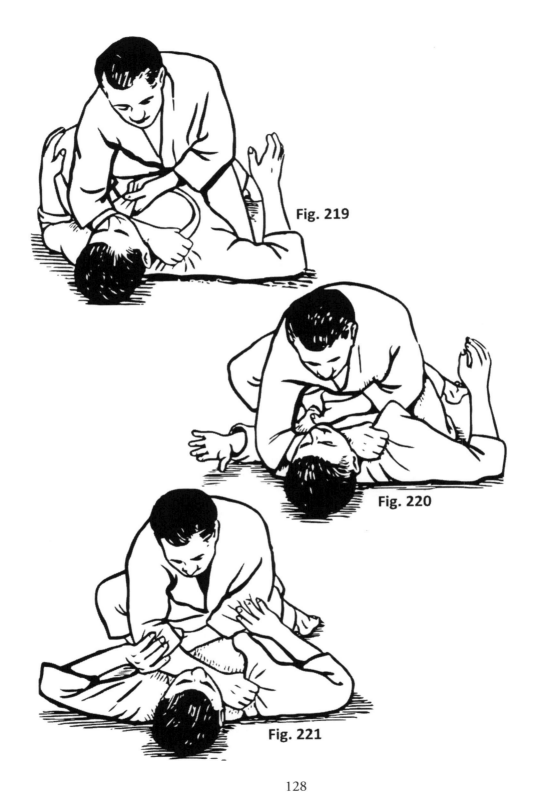

Fig. 219

Fig. 220

Fig. 221

The weakness of this lock lies in the ease with which your opponent can lessen pressure on his throat by bracing his arm against them at and thrusting up against your right elbow (Fig. 221). You can counter this to some extent, however, by leaning forward and rolling your right forearm anti-clockwise so that the little finger cutting-edge bears upwards towards the top of his head. At the same time lower your head as in Figure 212 and press diagonally down towards his throat.

Single Wing Choke (Katahajime)

This is applied against an opponent who turns his back on you when you are both struggling on the ground. For the purpose of illustration, I am assuming your opponent with is sitting upright his back towards you as in Figure 222, but the choke is, of course, no less from effective when made the lying position.

Pass your right arm round his neck and grasp the far collar of his jacket as round as you can comfortably reach. The palm of the hand should be down and the thumb cutting-edge of your forearm contact with his throat(Fig. 223). Pass your left arm round and under his left arm and press the palm or little finger edge of your left hand against the back of his head (Fig. 223). The lock is applied by pulling your right arm back against his throat while pushing forward with your left (Fig. 224). The more your opponent struggles to free his left arm the more he applies the choke against himself.

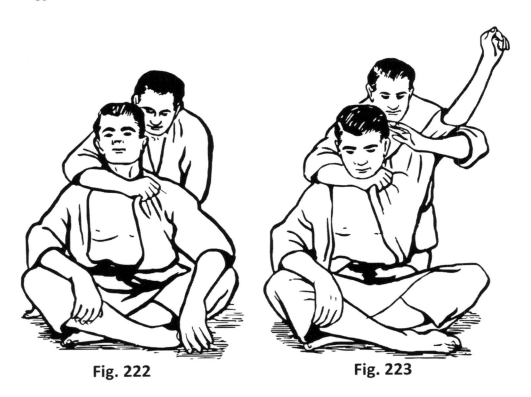

Fig. 222   **Fig. 223**

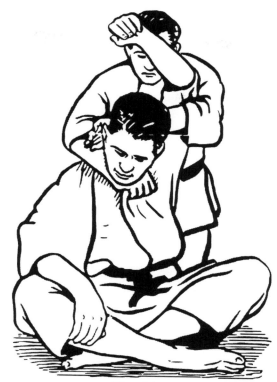

Fig. 224

The Naked Choke (Hadakajime)

So called because this choke can be equally well applied to a naked man since the jacket plays no part in its execution. Apart from this, it bears a close resemblance to the Single Wing in theory and effect.

Pass your right arm round his neck and bring the hand back towards you so that it grasps your left arm just above the elbow (Figs. 225 & 226). Now place the palm or little finger edge of your left hand against the back of your opponent's head, pressing forward with it while pulling back with the other (Fig. 227). The thumb cutting-edge of the right forearm (much nearer to the elbow than in the other chokes and strangles) presses against his throat.

Fig. 225

132

Fig. 226

Fig. 227

CHAPTER XII
Armlocks

A sound knowledge of armlocks is an effective weapon in any judoka's armoury because, used to proper advantage, they can turn a man who is no better than a modest performer in other departments of the sport into a redoubtable contest man.

Despite this, armlocks are surprisingly neglected in contest judo; mostly, I suspect, because the contestants are too slow in spotting opportunities for using them. Even in contests between Black Belts it is frequently possible to point to wasted chances in this direction.

A valuable object lesson can be gained if you and a partner lie on the mat and move about as if you were in semi-slow-motion contest together. Now, if you remember that the chance of an armlock occurs whenever your opponent's elbow moves away from his side, you will see just how often this opportunity presents itself. It remains for you but to seize on every such opening, and this you can only do from constant watchful practice, and from watching others practice.

Armlocks fall into three categories—two against a straight arm thrust out towards you (Fig. 228), and the third against a bent arm, usually when your opponent is pulling you or when he is trying to escape from a straight armlock (Fig. 229).

Fig. 228

Fig. 229

The Straight Armlock between the Thighs (Udehishige-Jujigatame)

In contest judo this lock is often used as an immediate follow-up to a throw. Alternatively, it may be made from your opponent's side, or from astride his body. The side position is shown in Figure 230. Your opponent is lying on his back and you are kneeling at his right side. Probably you have just attempted to strangle him but have failed because he managed to thwart you with his right arm.

Grasp his defending arm at the wrist with both hands and pull the arm to its full extent, his thumb away from you (Fig. 230). At the same time slide your left leg round his head so that it is immediately above his throat (Fig. 231). Now, bringing your right foot close under his body, roll over backwards so that you are almost sitting on your right heel. Maintain the tension on his right arm.

When rolling backwards cant your body slightly towards his head as by so doing his arm will be more effectively locked against your right thigh and, incidentally, the position will be more comfortable for you. Apply the lock by pulling his arm straight out and raising your hips (Fig. 232) and bearing down on his wrist and forearm. It is essential to keep his thumb uppermost to ensure that the pressure is applied in the correct direction against the elbow joint of the arm. You must also be close enough to him for your thigh to act as a fulcrum against his elbow. If your thigh is not high enough up his arm, he may be able to brace his elbow against it.

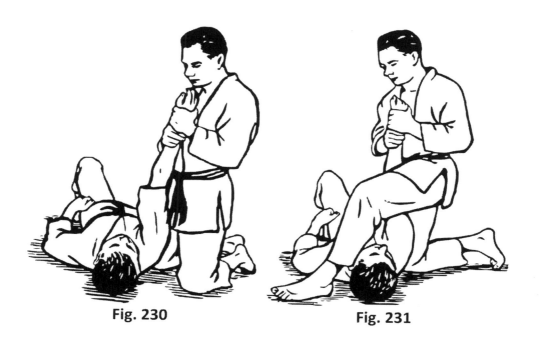

Fig. 230　　　　　　　　**Fig. 231**

Figure 233 shows the astride position of this lock. Opponent tries to ward you off with his right arm as you sit astride him. Grasp his defending arm at the wrist with both hands and roll to your left if, as in the illustration, it is his right arm you are holding. Your right leg must press close against your opponent's bod y to prevent him from rolling to his left to escape.

Your left leg is close up against his right side, possibly under it a little, your buttocks as near as comfort will allow to your left heel. Bear his extended arm down across your left thigh (Fig. 234). Your victim's thumb must be kept uppermost to ensure that the pressure is applied in correct direction against the elbow joint.

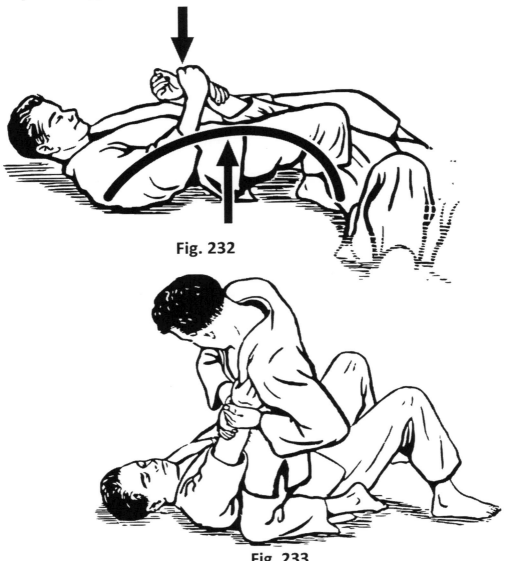

Fig. 232

Fig. 233

Fig. 234

The Lock from a Throw (Udehishige-Jujigatame)

If in the course of practicing this lock you lose your balance, you must immediately release your hold of your opponent's arm. Failure to do so may result in painful injury.

In this instance, you have thrown your opponent but not convincingly enough to be awarded a point. You are now standing at his right side holding his right sleeve in your left hand (Fig. 235). At once grip his wrist with your other hand, pull his arm up straight and bring your right foot close to his side if it is not already there. Do not relax your pull on his arm.

Now sit down close to your right heel, placing your left foot at the far side of his neck, as you do so (Fig. 236) and still maintaining the pull on his arm. As you reach the mat roll back and apply the lock across your right thigh. The lock will be the more effective if you take a convenient opportunity to change the grip of your left hand from his sleeve to his forearm (Fig. 237).

Fig. 235

Fig. 236

138

Fig. 237

Straight Armlock from Astride Opponent (Udekujiki)

This Straight Armlock from Astride Your Opponent is simpler than the one applied across the thigh but is less frequently used in contest for the simple reason that the opportunity for its use occurs less often. One of the basic principles of judo groundwork is always to keep your elbows close to your sides. The beginner who forgets this precept and commits the error of straightening an arm to push his opponent away provides the perfect situation for an armlock. In Fig. 238 you are astride your opponent. Your attempts to defeat him with a Normal Cross Strangle have failed because of his persistent and successful efforts to relieve the pressure on his neck. He now attempts to hold you off with his right arm. As he does so, grasp his wrist with both hands and pull his arm out to its full extent. At the same time slide you r left leg out at an angle to his body and immobilize his arm against your thigh (Fig. 239). It is important that his thumb should be uppermost and the fulcrum provided by you r thigh should be nearer his shoulder than his elbow. If your thigh is below his elbow, he will brace his arm against it and escape.

This lock can also be applied using the attacker's knee as the fulcrum. See Figure 240.

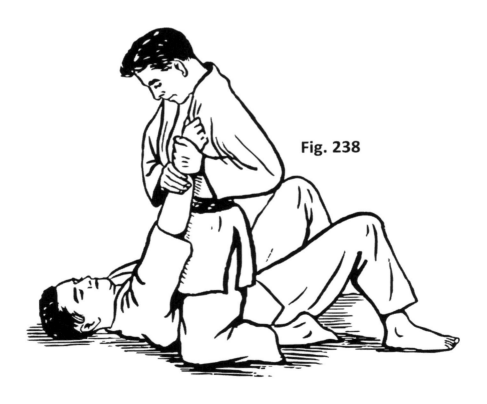

Fig. 238

Fig. 239

Fig. 240

141

Straight Armlock from Beneath Opponent (*Gyaku Udekujiki*)

This is not an easy lock to execute and is included here principally to illustrate that the man on top is not necessarily in the position of advantage.

You are lying on your back and your opponent is attacking you from above. Your chance lies in maneuvering yourself so that your legs are on either side of your opponent's body. If your opponent is alert, he will prevent or escape from this vulnerable position, but often he is so absorbed in trying to attack you with some sort of neck-lock that he fails to notice his danger.

As he reaches forward towards your neck, grasp his right wrist and pull it up to your shoulder (Fig. 241). At the same time bring up your right leg and plant the sole of your foot firmly into his left thigh. Straighten your leg and push his thigh from under him. The opposing pull on his arm and the thrust of his thigh will bring him full length to the mat. As he falls, roll over to your right and swing your outstretched left leg over his upper right arm (Fig. 242), if possible anchoring your foot under his head or neck.

Apply the lock by bearing down on his arm with your leg and lifting with your hands. In this case, since you are below your opponent, his right hand should point to the ground, thumb downwards.

Fig. 241

Fig. 242

The Figure Four Armlock (Udegarami)

So called because your arm and his together form a figure four when the lock is correctly applied.

Your opponent is on his back and you are kneeling at his left side (Fig. 243). He reaches up with his right hand to push you away and you attempt a straight armlock. He tries to escape this by bending his arm, and you reply by gripping his wrist with you r right hand and driving it down to the mat, pinning his body beneath your own as you do so (Fig. 244). Anchor his arm, palm of hand uppermost, firmly to the mat above the level of the shoulder, and pass your left arm under his upper arm to grip your own right wrist (Fig. 245). Take care that your arm passes under his arm close up to his shoulder well above the elbow. Your right hand meanwhile pulls his right arm round the top of his head towards his left shoulder to make the angle between his fore and upper arms less than a right angle.

Apply the lock by holding down with your right hand and lifting with your left. A refinement is to turn your left wrist in an anti-clockwise direction in order to bring the thumb cutting-edge of your forearm against his upper arm.

143

Figure 245 illustrates a slight variation in the technique described above. In this case the attacker has brought his right arm under this opponent's neck instead of over it. This method is just as effective.

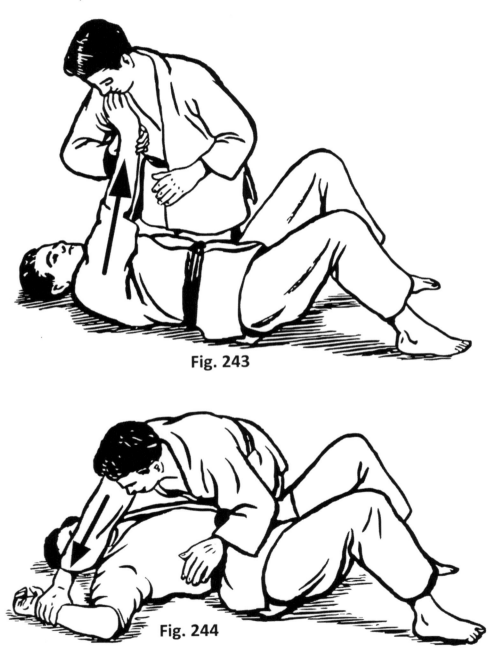

Fig. 243

Fig. 244

Fig. 245

The Arm Crush (Ude Appaku-Suru)

This is the third of the Armlock group and is not generally well known. It is surprising that it should not be better known as it is a simple lock to use and markedly effective.

You are sitting astride your opponent and he pushes at you with his right arm. You reply by encircling his arm with your left arm, pressing against his upper arm with the thumb cutting-edge of your forearm (Fig. 246). Now roll over to your left so that you are sitting close to your left heel. As you do so, lock the fingers of your two hands together, and retain control of his body by pressing it down on the ground with your right leg (Fig. 247). The lock becomes increasingly effective as you roll further to your left and the weight of your body comes on to his arm.

Press directly upwards with your left forearm, assisted by your right hand. The upward thrust of the cutting-edge of your forearm on the muscles of his upper arm should bring quick submission.

Fig. 248 shows an alternative method in which the opponent's jacket is gripped instead of the two hands being clasped. In my opinion it is the less effective of the two.

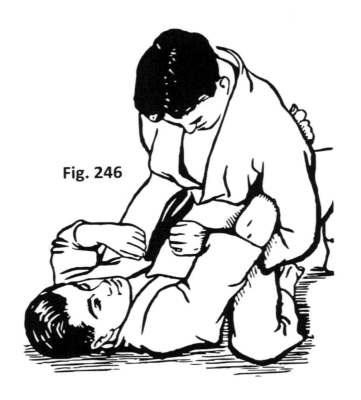

Fig. 246

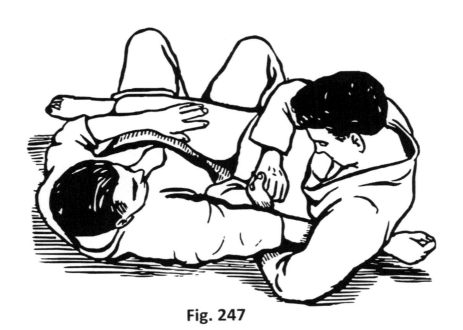

Fig. 247

146

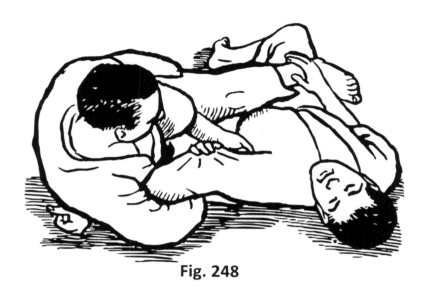

Fig. 248

A Final Note on Armlocks

In the course of hard practice and keen contests one's hands tend to become wet and slippery, making it difficult to retain a commanding grip of the opponent's wrist. For this reason, I prefer the technique shown in Figure 235, whenever practicable. In this it will be seen the attacker is gripping his opponent's sleeve with his left hand, the material offering him a much more secure hold. At the last moment, of course, as will be seen in Figure 236, the left hand is transferred to the opponent's wrist in order to complete the lock.

Printed in Great Britain
by Amazon